א מנין יידן : און אנדערע זאכן

A MINYEN YIDN

(UN ANDERE ZAKHN)

A BUNCH OF JEWS
(AND OTHER STUFF)

By Max B. Perlson
& Trina Robbins

Bedside PRESS

Translated into English from Yiddish by Hershl Hartman.

Cover illustration by Barbara Mendes
Design & Typography by Relish New Brand Experience
Second printing through CreateSpace

LIBRARY AND ARCHIVES CANADA CATALOGUING IN PUBLICATION

Robbins, Trina, author
A minyen Yidn (un andere zakhn) = A bunch of Jews (and other stuff) / Trina Robbins.

Originally published in Yiddish as a collection of short stories by Max Perlson under title A minyen Yidn. Translated into English, then adapted into a graphic novel format by Trina Robbins and a variety of artists.
Edited by Hope Nicholson.
Illustrators include Barbara Mendes, Miriam Libicki, Shary Flenniken, Eve Fuchgott, Anne Timmons, Miriam Katin, Ken Steacy, Joan Steacy.
Issued in print and electronic formats.
ISBN 978-0-9939970-5-1 (softcover).--ISBN 978-1-988715-00-1 (PDF)

1. Perlson, Max--Comic books, strips, etc. 2. Jews--Belarus--Social life and customs--Anecdotes--Comic books, strips, etc. 3. Jews, Belarusian--New York (State)--New York--Social life and customs--Anecdotes--Comic books, strips, etc. 4. Jewish journalists--New York (State)--New York--Biography--Comic books, strips, etc. 5. Jews--Belarus--Biography--Comic books, strips, etc. 6. Jews, Belarusian--New York (State)--New York--Biography--Comic books, strips, etc. 7. Brooklyn (New York, N.Y.)--History--Anecdotes. 8. Comics adaptations. I. Nicholson, Hope, 1986-, editor II. Perlson, Max. Minyen Yidn. III. Title. IV. Title: Bunch of Jews (and other stuff).

DS113.8.B44R63 2017 974.7'230049240478 C2017-900337-2
C2017-900338-0

BEDSIDE PRESS
http://bedsidepress.com

To my dear wife, Bessie Rosenman Perlson,
— a teacher in a New York public school —
whom I have to thank for the fact that this
booklet has seen the light of day.
M. B. PERLSON, MAY, 1938

To my wonderful daughter,
Casey Kahney-Robbins, for finding this lost book.
Thank you!
TRINA ROBBINS

With many thanks to Hershl Hartman for his translation
of the original text from Yiddish into English.

Thanks to Saida Temofonte for her lettering
assistance in selected stories.

PLATINUM FUNDERS

Aaron Cohen
AC
Aditya Bidikar
Adrienne Figus
Agnès L.
Alex Pacheco-West
Alexander Ostroff
Alexandra S.
Alexandra T. Herzog
Alexis Aaeng
Alison Knight
Amanda Graff
Andrea Smith
Andrea Villa
Andrew Belding
Andy Kolovos
annlarabee@gmail.com
Anonymous
Archigan
Aron Silverstone
Arthur Green
Arwen Jean Fleming
Ashleigh Hamilton Cole
Bekki Ann
Ben Lieberman
Ben Perkins
Bill Kraut
Bitsy
Bobb Waller
Brian Fried
Bryan J. Reigate
Brydon Caldwell
Candida Rifkind
Caress Redd
Carl Rigney
Carlos Duarte Do Nascimento
Carol G. Russak
Carol L Tilley
Carolyn Potts
Cathy Green
Catie Coleman
Chad Shipley
Chip Mosher
Chris Marquardson
Chris Plakholm
Christopher Bilbo
Christopher Day
Colin Eles
Comikaza
Connie Tolleson
Conor Bendle

Cosmic Monkey Comics
Crystal M Rollins
Dan Hoizner
Dan Theodore
Dani Shuping
Daniel Korn
Dar Blue & Anne V
Darren Duncan
Dave Baxter
David Broyles
David Greenberg
David Lasky
David Macpherson
David Walter
DC Fleming
Debbi Jones
Dennis F. Rogers
Denys Howard
Diana Green
Dominiquea22@yahoo.com
Donald E. Claxon
Donna Brearcliffe
Doug Goldschmidt
Doug O'Loughlin –
    Comic Cave
Doug Rednour
Douglas Dollars
Drew Ford
D-Rock
Dybbuk Klezmer
Ed White
Eitan Kensky
Elaine Blank
Elisheva Bailey
Ella Libicki Feldman
Elliot Blake
Erica "Vulpinfox" Schmitt
Erik Norman Berglund
Erin Allison Stedman
Erin Subramanian
Eva Konigsberg
Evan Ritchie
Eve Furchgott
Florian Schiffmann
Francesca Garrett
Frank Martin Smith IV
Frankie Mundens
Fred Herman
Fred Van Lente
Fred W Johnson
Gabriel Schlesinger

Gail de Vos
Gary Gaines
Gavi Raab
Gianluca Glazer
Gina Curtice
Greg "schmegs" Schwartz
Greg Pak
Greg Tanner
Hailey Conner
hal niedzviecki
Hannah Fattor
Happy Harbor Comics
Holly Williams
Howard Fein
Hoyt Day
Ian Leong
Isaac 'Will It Work' Dansicker
Ivan Salazar
Izzy Ladinsky
J. F. Wallace
J. Hill
Jaci Dahlvang
Jacque Nodell
Jaimie Noy
Jake Zirkle
James Kaplan
Janet Hetherington
Janice M. Eisen
Janna Silverstein
Jason Franks
Jay Lofstead
JayJay Jackson
Jedidjah de Vries
Jeff Labrack
Jeff Metzner
Jeff Newelt
Jeff Rowat
jeichlerlevine@gmail.com
Jen Savage
Jennifer Young
Jenny Caplan
Jenny Schwartzberg
Jeremy Ladan
Jerry Feldstein
Jesse Post
Jessi Jordan
Jessica Bader
Jessica Berglund
Jessica Kirzane
Jim Finlay
Jim Kosmicki

Jimmy Palmiotti
Joe Herman
John Alfred Young
John K Snyder III
john newquist
john siuntres
Jon Bocknek
Jonathan Edwards
Jonathan L. Miller
Jordan Thomas
Jordana Greenblatt
Julia Round
Julia Trocme-Latter
Julie Isen
K Nisenshal
Kaja Hanson
Karen Akiba
Karen Gillmore
Karen Green
Kari Maaren
Kat and Jason Romero
Kate Moss
Kelly Tindall
Kernes Family
Keshav Sapru
Kim MacDonald
Kirk & Mindy Spencer
Kristin Evenson Hirst
Kristy Quinn
Landers
Larry Yudelson
Laura C. Morales
Lauren Ross-Feldman
Lawrence Manekin
LEGENDS COMICS & BOOKS
Len Dvorkin
Lennhoff Family
Linda Bernard
Lizzette Walls
Lois Athena Buhalis
M. Brett
Maarten Daalder
Madeline Hartman
Mainon A Schwartz
Marcelle Kosman
Margaret St. John
Marianne
Mariusz Kałczewiak and
    Irad Ben Isaak
Mark Byzewski
Mark Hickernell

Mark Tague
Mark Tomko
Matthew Barnett
Meg Crane
Michael A. Burstein
Michael Gravely
Michael Kurland
Michail Dim. Drakomathioulakis
Michele S
MIchelle Katz
Michelle Reid
Mike "ComicsDC" Rhode
Mike Brown
Mike Meltzer
Mike Mitchell
Mikey Silverstein
mirra.neiman@gmail.com
Molly J. Scanlon
Moshe Feder
MOSHE PRIGAN
msappel
Nanna Sally Nelson
Natalie B. Litofsky
Natalie Hasell
Natasha A.
Neil LaPointe
Nichoas Burns
Nick & Elizabeth Holub
Nina Lehman
Noah Lesgold
Norman Jaffe
Nyala Ali
Pattie Miller
Paul Daniel
Paul F Engelberg
Peter Mazzeo
Peter Young
Philip F
Pulp Literature Press
R Bruce MacKeen
R.J.H.
Randy Wood
Ray Powell
Raymond Larrett
Rebecca Wachter
Richard Flores
Rifkah Epner
Rivqa Rafael
Rob D. Atwood
Robert Early
Robert J. Plass

Robert Kollenberg
Robert Pincombe
Roberta
RobJD
Roger B.A. Klorese & David Haney
Rose Lemberg and Bogi Takács
Ryan French
Sami
Sarah Bricker
Sarah Kadish
Scott Harriman
Sean McGinley
Sharyn November
Shmuel Gowicz
sirshannon
Sophia Bisignano-Vadino
Staci Lichterman
Stan MacDonald
Stan!
Stephane PHILIPPO
Stéphane T.
Stephanie Carey
Stephanie Noell
Steven E. Rowe
Steven Schaffer
Stig Olsen
Strange Adventures Comix
    & Curiosities
Sue-Rae Rosenfeld
Susan S.
Svend Andersen
Sylvia Allen
Ted, Leo, and Desmond Sobel
Terence Fuller
Terri Thal
Terry Howard
thatraja
Tim Hanley
Todd Good
Tomer Gurantz
Torrey Podmajersky
Tove Heikkinen
Travis Seifman
Trevor Ashfield
Tuvyah Dov
V. Garlock
Valancia Clark
Vicki Hsu
William Davis
Zinn Loren
Zvi Jankelowitz

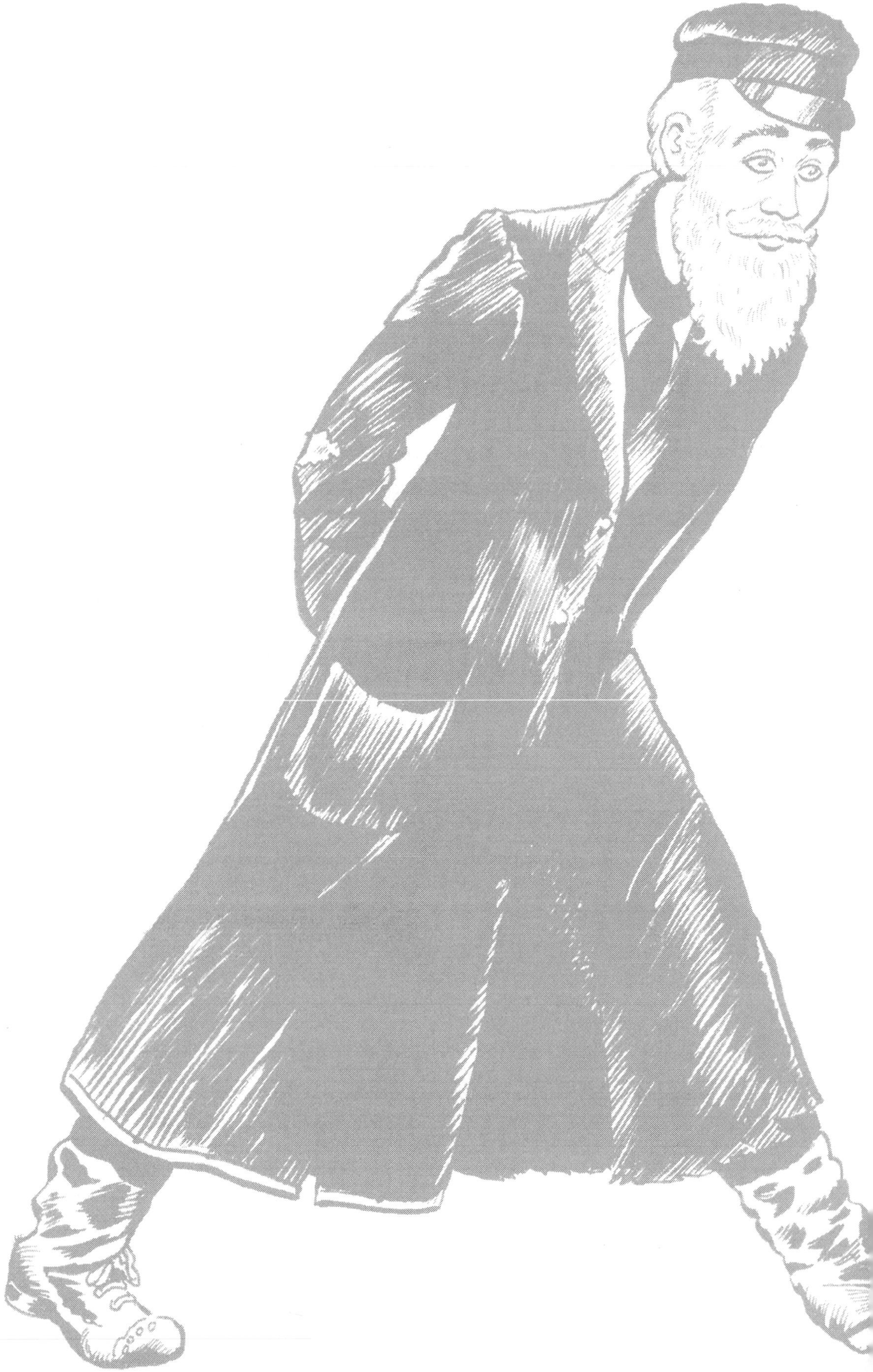

CONTENTS

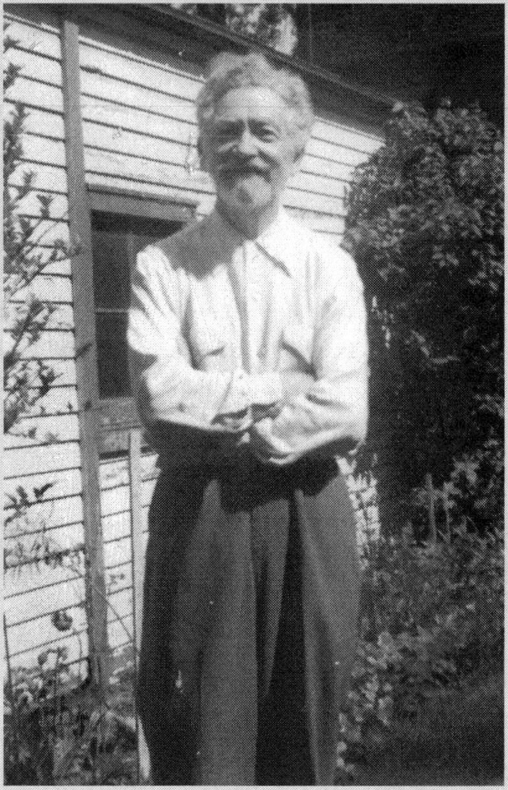

Max B. Perlson

The family in Duboy. *Standing, left to right*: unknown relative and the brothers Fischel, Mutye, Itzak. *Sitting, left to right*: Father Elja, sister Rochele, mother Trayne.

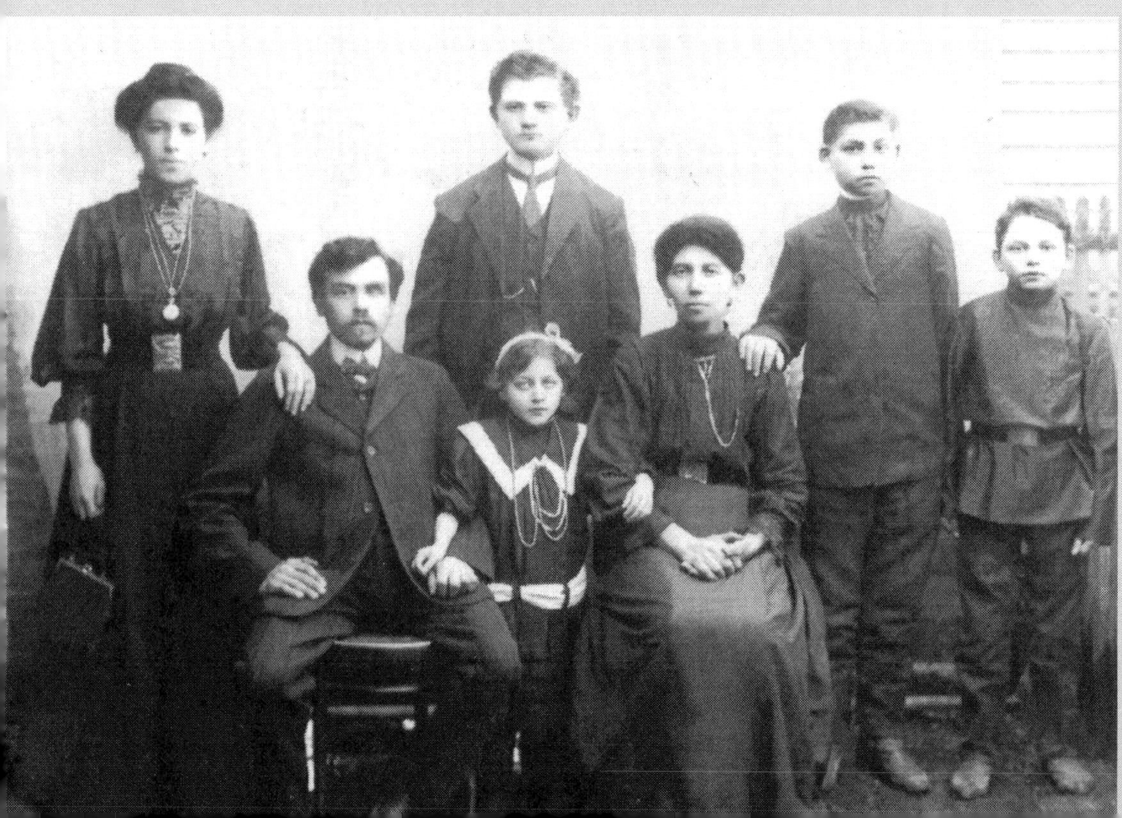

Of an Ungrateful Daughter and a Lost Book Found

TRINA ROBBINS

MY FATHER, MAX B. PERLSON (Mutl or Mutye to his friends), grew up in what is now Belarus, in a tiny shtetl called Duboy. He came to this country all alone at the age of sixteen, attended night school, and learned English. He learned well; our home was filled with books, all of which he had read, and because they were around, I read them too. Among them I remember the complete Mark Twain, Dickens, the poems of William Blake and John Keats, the memoirs, god help us, of Ulysses S. Grant. And he wrote. But he wrote in Yiddish. He contributed articles to Yiddish language papers like The Forward and The Tog, and in 1938 he published a book called *A Minyen Yidn un Andere Zakhn*, which I have loosely translated as *A Bunch of Jews and Other Stuff*.

I loved my parents. My second grade schoolteacher mother taught me to read and write at the age of four, and my father took me on countless visits to the Brooklyn Museum and the Prospect Park botanical garden. But I distanced myself from his Yiddish writing. I wanted him to be *American*. Yiddish was *foreign*. I was embarrassed, no, *ashamed* of his Yiddish writing, and as a result I ignored it, and never knew or cared what his book might be about.

Fast forward sixty years or so. Both my parents were long gone, and so, I was convinced, was my father's book. What could be more obscure than a book in Yiddish, published in 1938? It was lost forever, never to be found again.

But I didn't reckon on my daughter, a much better daughter than I had been, and I didn't reckon on the internet. She found *A Minyen Yidn*, reprinted at ABE Books! I ordered a bunch of copies, for me and for her. And she found the Jewish Library in Brooklyn, which aims to collect all the Yiddish books that exist, and the Jewish library turned out to have *two* original copies of my father's book. And they sold me one! And through the Jewish library I found a translator, the fabulous Hershl Hartman.

I finally got to read my father's book, and loved what I read. It was a collection of short pieces, almost verbal snapshots, of the people he grew up with in Duboy, with more snapshots at the end, taking place in Brooklyn and the Lower East Side, where he lived after coming to America. The stories are for the most part funny. There's a series of Jewish folk tales about a mythical shtetl called Chelm, where everybody is astonishingly dimwitted, and often in his stories Duboy sounds a lot like Chelm. Apparently not everybody who read the book had my father's sense of humor. My father was one of a group of men who had all immigrated from Duboy at around the same time, and they called themselves the Duboier Young Men's Progressive Association, although past a certain point they were no longer "young men." According to my big sister, Harriet, who, five years older than me, was more aware of these things, some of his fellow immigrants were furious at my father for his depictions. It got to the point where he didn't dare come to meetings of the group, because as Harriet put it, "It was a case of hang him high."

Reading the stories that had once so horrified my father's fellow immigrants, I realized the book was perfect material for adapting into comic form, and that's what I did. I made a hopeful wish list of cartoonists who I thought would illustrate the stories perfectly, and to my everlasting joy, most of them said they'd love to. It has been an immense pleasure to see their finished pages arrive one by one, to see how each artist interprets my script and my father's story, each differently and each beautifully.

Cover artist Barbara "Willy" Mendes has been my friend since 1969. There was a time when she and I were the only two women in San Francisco drawing comics. She now lives in Los Angeles, where she has a gallery full of her vibrant art. To be honest, Willy was my second choice for a cover artist. I really wanted Chagall, but he was unavailable.

As for my publisher, Bedside Press, I've known Hope Nicholson since she got in touch with me when she was reprinting the Golden Age Canadian superheroine, Nelvana of the Northern Lights, 1 year before I finally met her in person at the Toronto Comics Arts Festival in 2014. I'm a proud contributor to her immensely successful anthology, *The Secret Loves of Geek Girls*, and I'm honored to be a member of her group of women comic creators, who meet poolside each year at the San Diego comic convention. She wears bright red lipstick and beautiful vintage frocks. Almost before I finished telling Hope about my father's book, she told me she'd like to publish it. She has been my steadfast publisher and co-editor, she has advised me wisely and I have complained and cried on her shoulder electronically. Thank you, Hope!

And thanks to everyone who made this book what it is. I hope you, the reader, like it. I hope my father likes it, and that I have atoned, just a wee bit, for being the wretched ungrateful daughter I was.

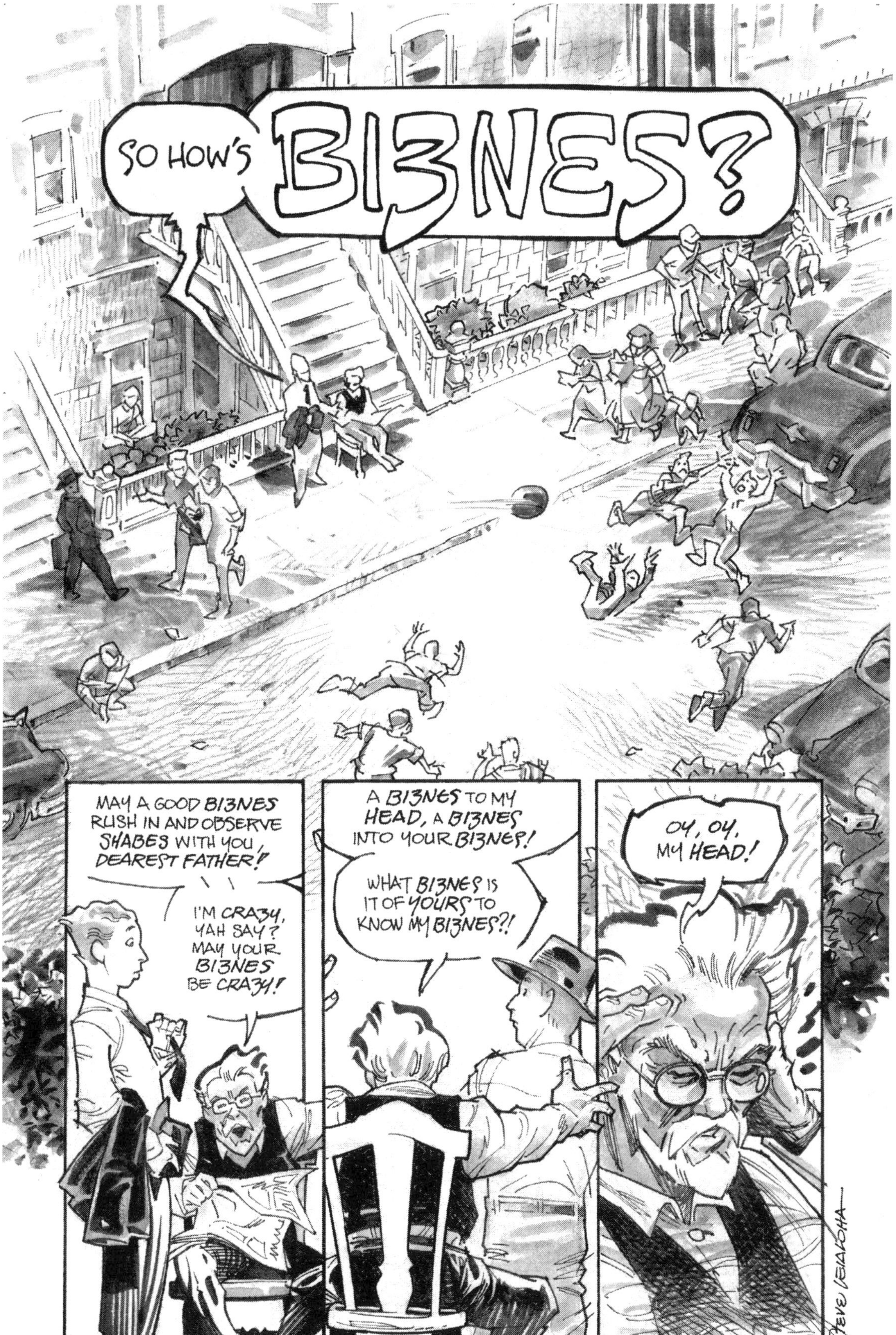
SO HOW'S BIZNES?
MAY A GOOD BIZNES RUSH IN AND OBSERVE SHABES WITH YOU, DEAREST FATHER!
I'M CRAZY, YAH SAY? MAY YOUR BIZNES BE CRAZY!
A BIZNES TO MY HEAD, A BIZNES INTO YOUR BIZNES!
WHAT BIZNES IS IT OF YOURS TO KNOW MY BIZNES?!
OY, OY, MY HEAD!
STEVE VEIALOHA

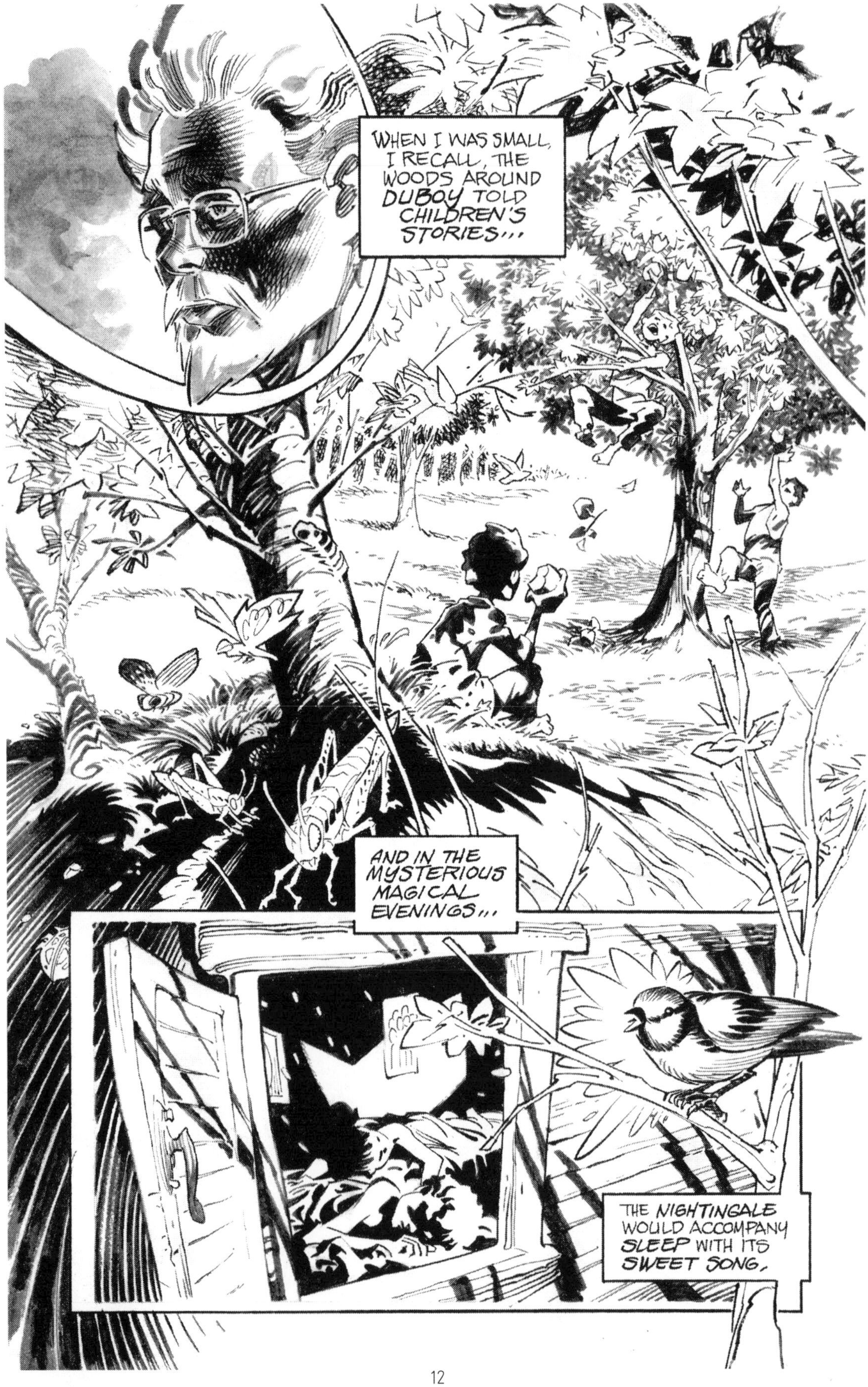
WHEN I WAS SMALL, I RECALL, THE WOODS AROUND DUBOY TOLD CHILDREN'S STORIES...
AND IN THE MYSTERIOUS MAGICAL EVENINGS...
THE NIGHTINGALE WOULD ACCOMPANY SLEEP WITH ITS SWEET SONG.

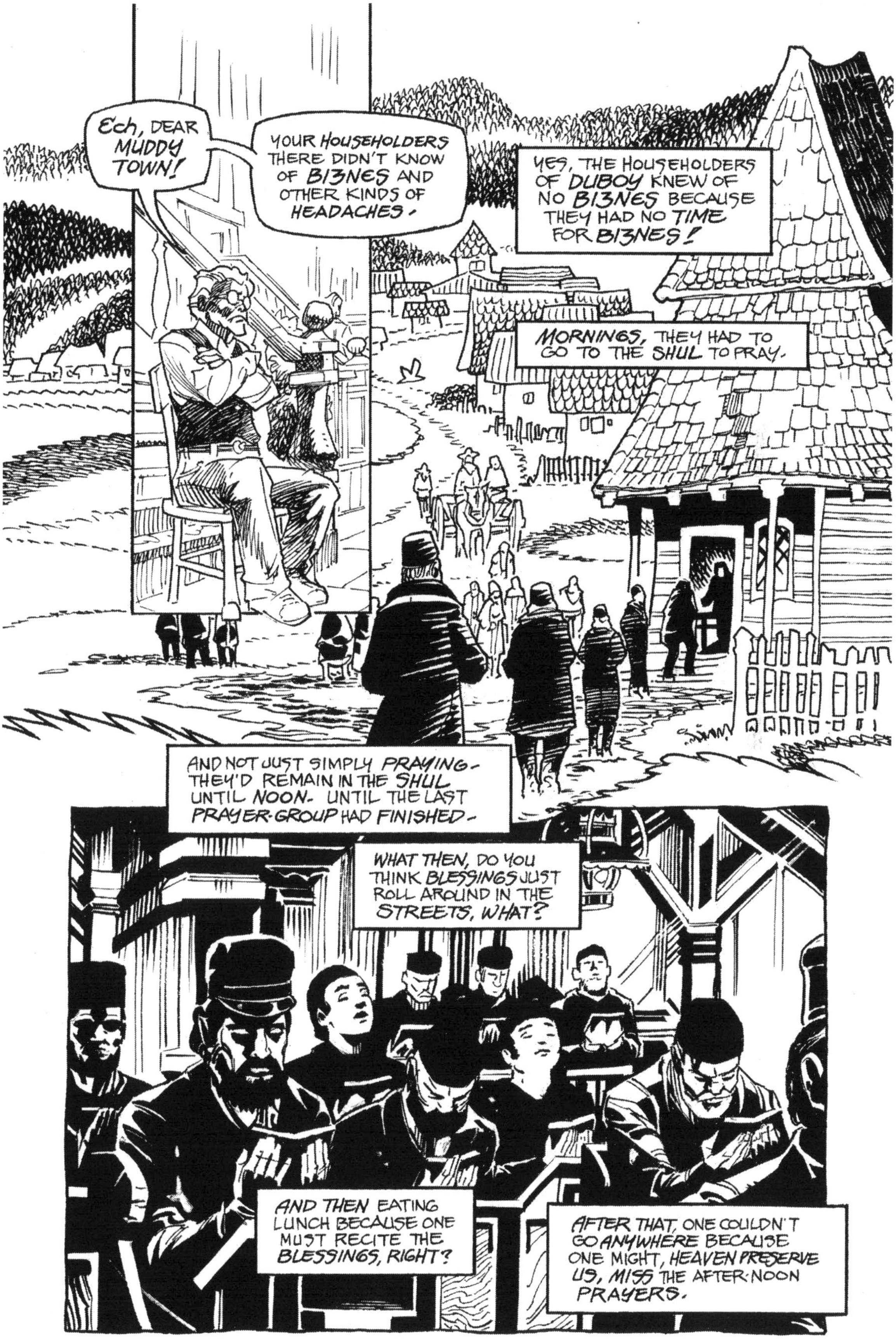
Ech, DEAR MUDDY TOWN!
YOUR HOUSEHOLDERS THERE DIDN'T KNOW OF BIZNES AND OTHER KINDS OF HEADACHES.
YES, THE HOUSEHOLDERS OF DUBOY KNEW OF NO BIZNES BECAUSE THEY HAD NO TIME FOR BIZNES!
MORNINGS, THEY HAD TO GO TO THE SHUL TO PRAY.
AND NOT JUST SIMPLY PRAYING- THEY'D REMAIN IN THE SHUL UNTIL NOON- UNTIL THE LAST PRAYER-GROUP HAD FINISHED-
WHAT THEN, DO YOU THINK BLESSINGS JUST ROLL AROUND IN THE STREETS, WHAT?
AND THEN EATING LUNCH BECAUSE ONE MUST RECITE THE BLESSINGS, RIGHT?
AFTER THAT, ONE COULDN'T GO ANYWHERE BECAUSE ONE MIGHT, HEAVEN PRESERVE US, MISS THE AFTER-NOON PRAYERS.

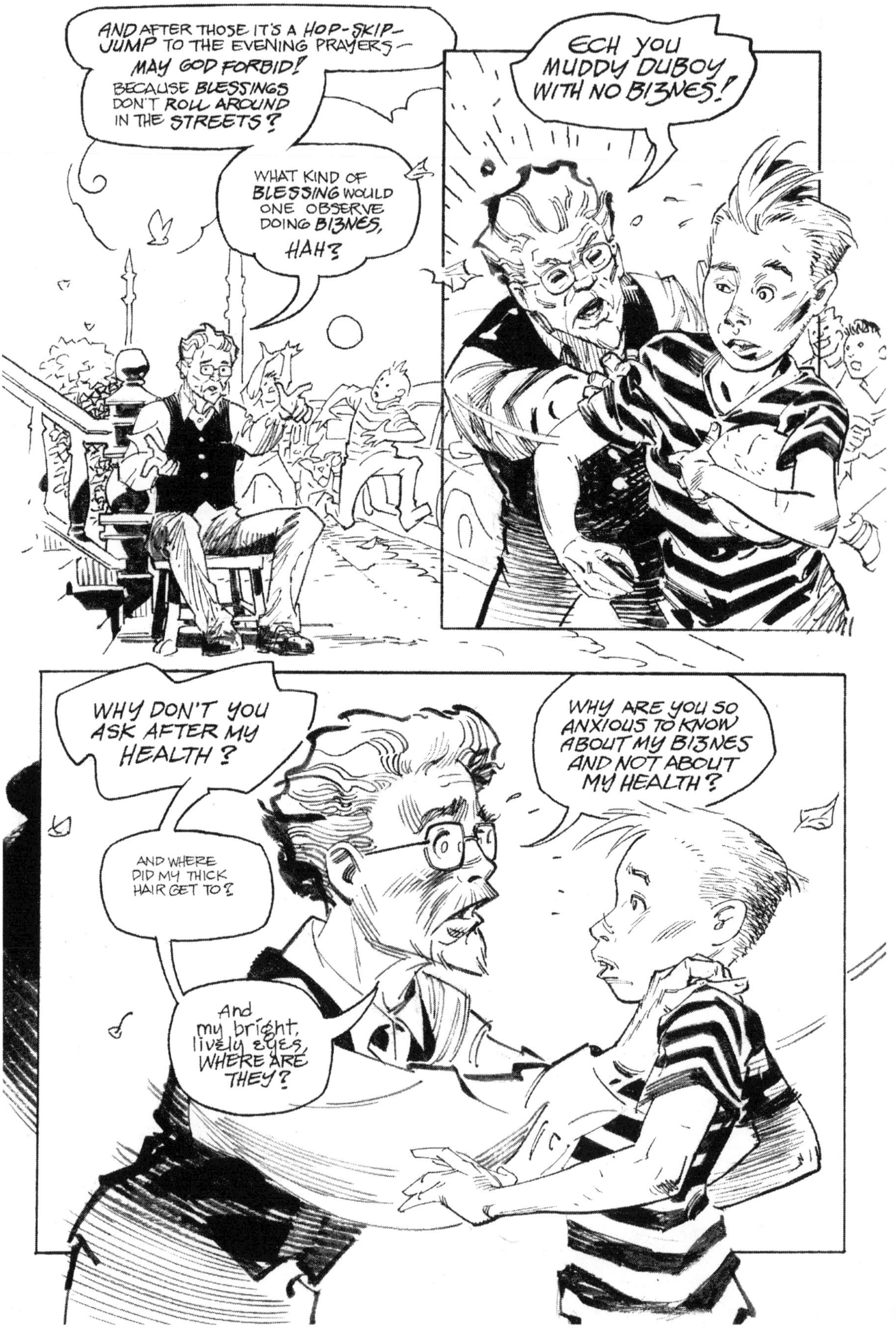
AND AFTER THOSE IT'S A HOP-SKIP-JUMP TO THE EVENING PRAYERS— MAY GOD FORBID! BECAUSE BLESSINGS DON'T ROLL AROUND IN THE STREETS?
WHAT KIND OF BLESSING WOULD ONE OBSERVE DOING BIZNES, HAH?
ECH YOU MUDDY DUBOY WITH NO BIZNES!
WHY DON'T YOU ASK AFTER MY HEALTH?
AND WHERE DID MY THICK HAIR GET TO?
And my bright, lively eyes, WHERE ARE THEY?
WHY ARE YOU SO ANXIOUS TO KNOW ABOUT MY BIZNES AND NOT ABOUT MY HEALTH?

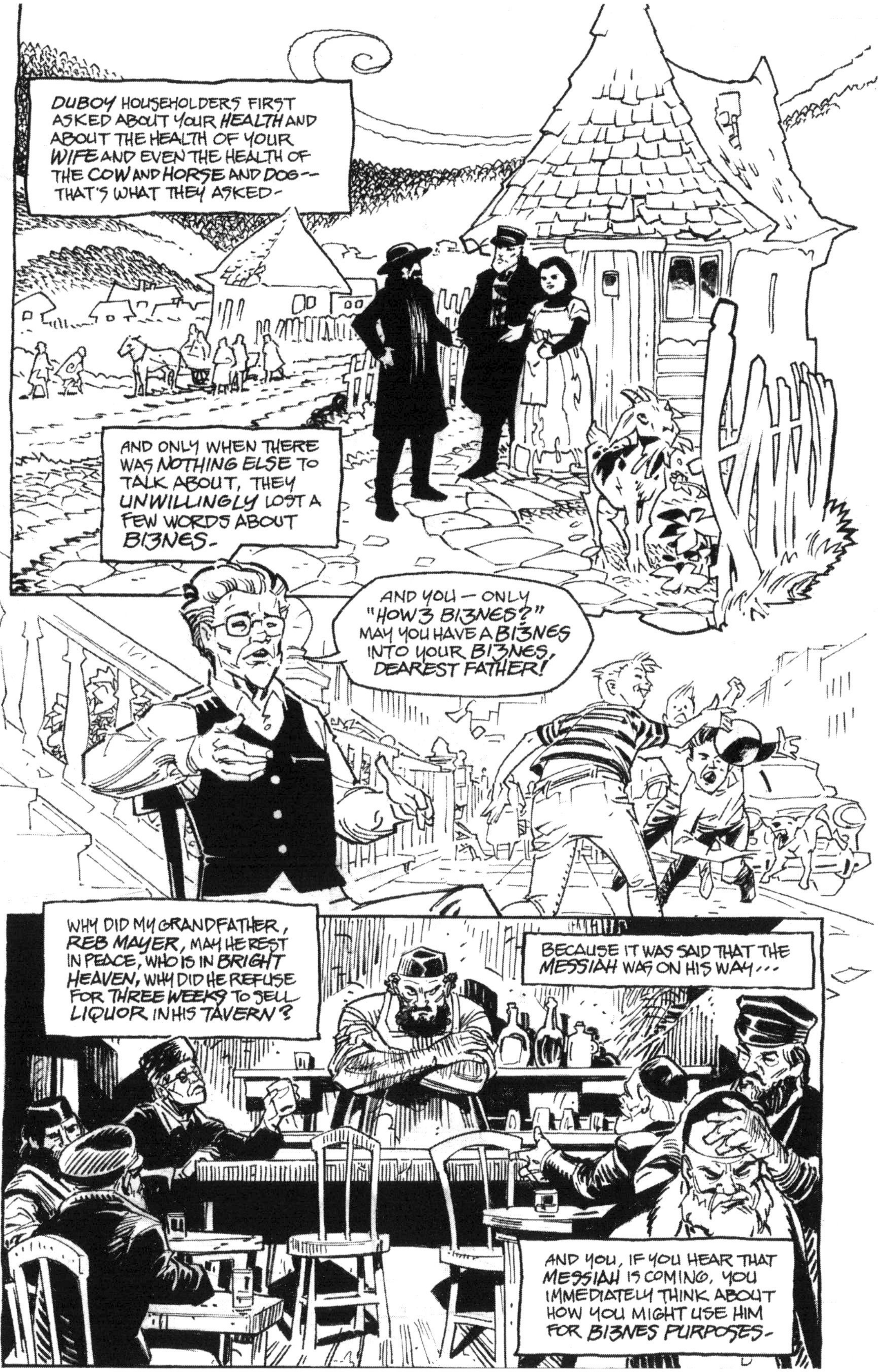
DUBOY HOUSEHOLDERS FIRST ASKED ABOUT YOUR HEALTH AND ABOUT THE HEALTH OF YOUR WIFE AND EVEN THE HEALTH OF THE COW AND HORSE AND DOG-- THAT'S WHAT THEY ASKED-
AND ONLY WHEN THERE WAS NOTHING ELSE TO TALK ABOUT, THEY UNWILLINGLY LOST A FEW WORDS ABOUT BIZNES-
AND YOU — ONLY "HOWZ BIZNES?" MAY YOU HAVE A BIZNES INTO YOUR BIZNES, DEAREST FATHER!
WHY DID MY GRANDFATHER, REB MAYER, MAY HE REST IN PEACE, WHO IS IN BRIGHT HEAVEN, WHY DID HE REFUSE FOR THREE WEEKS TO SELL LIQUOR IN HIS TAVERN?
BECAUSE IT WAS SAID THAT THE MESSIAH WAS ON HIS WAY...
AND YOU, IF YOU HEAR THAT MESSIAH IS COMING, YOU IMMEDIATELY THINK ABOUT HOW YOU MIGHT USE HIM FOR BIZNES PURPOSES-

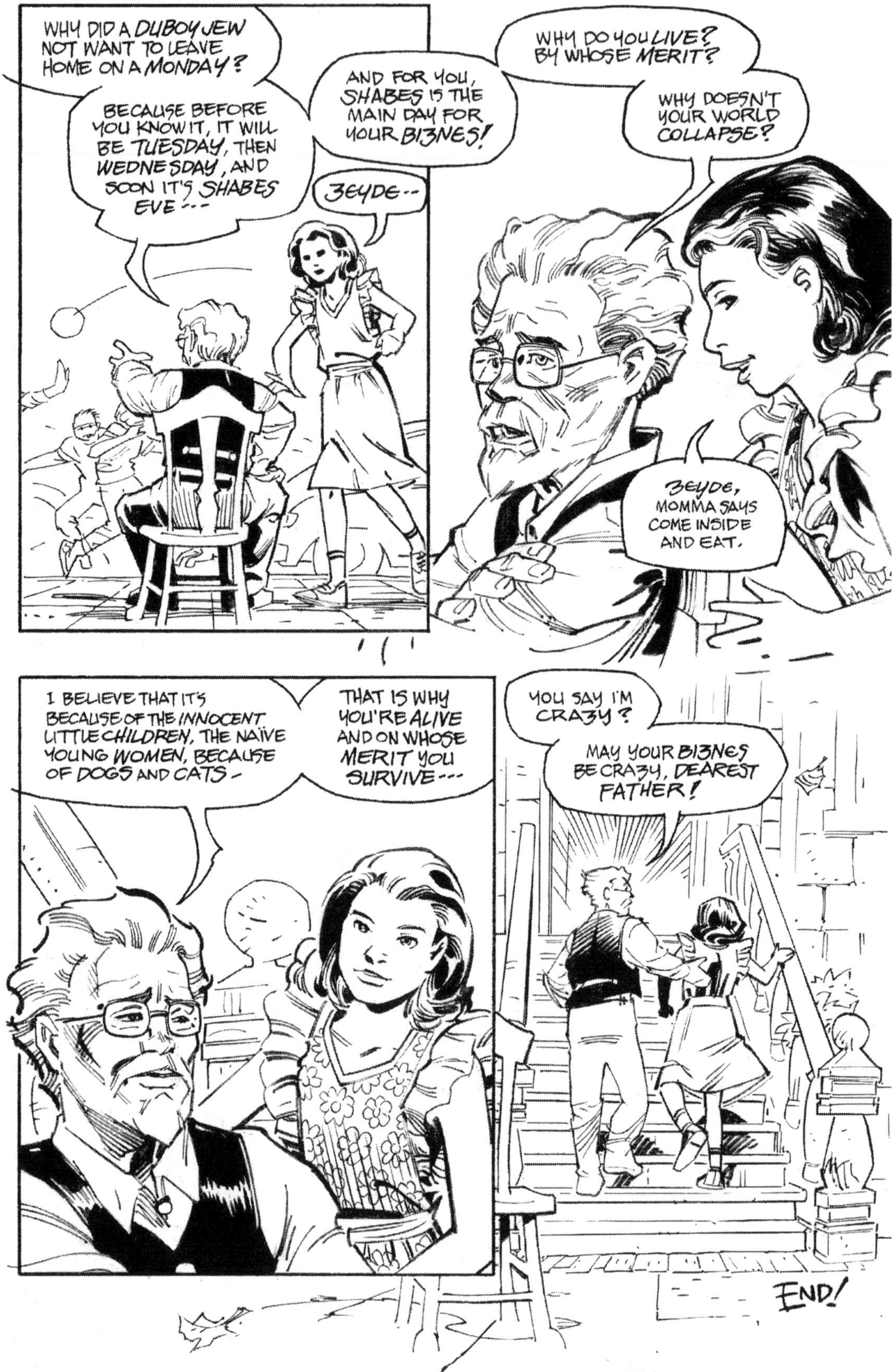
WHY DID A DUBOY JEW NOT WANT TO LEAVE HOME ON A MONDAY?
BECAUSE BEFORE YOU KNOW IT, IT WILL BE TUESDAY, THEN WEDNESDAY, AND SOON IT'S SHABES EVE---
AND FOR YOU, SHABES IS THE MAIN DAY FOR YOUR BIZNES!
ZEYDE--
WHY DO YOU LIVE? BY WHOSE MERIT?
WHY DOESN'T YOUR WORLD COLLAPSE?
ZEYDE, MOMMA SAYS COME INSIDE AND EAT.
I BELIEVE THAT IT'S BECAUSE OF THE INNOCENT LITTLE CHILDREN, THE NAÏVE YOUNG WOMEN, BECAUSE OF DOGS AND CATS-
THAT IS WHY YOU'RE ALIVE AND ON WHOSE MERIT YOU SURVIVE---
YOU SAY I'M CRAZY?
MAY YOUR BIZNES BE CRAZY, DEAREST FATHER!
END!

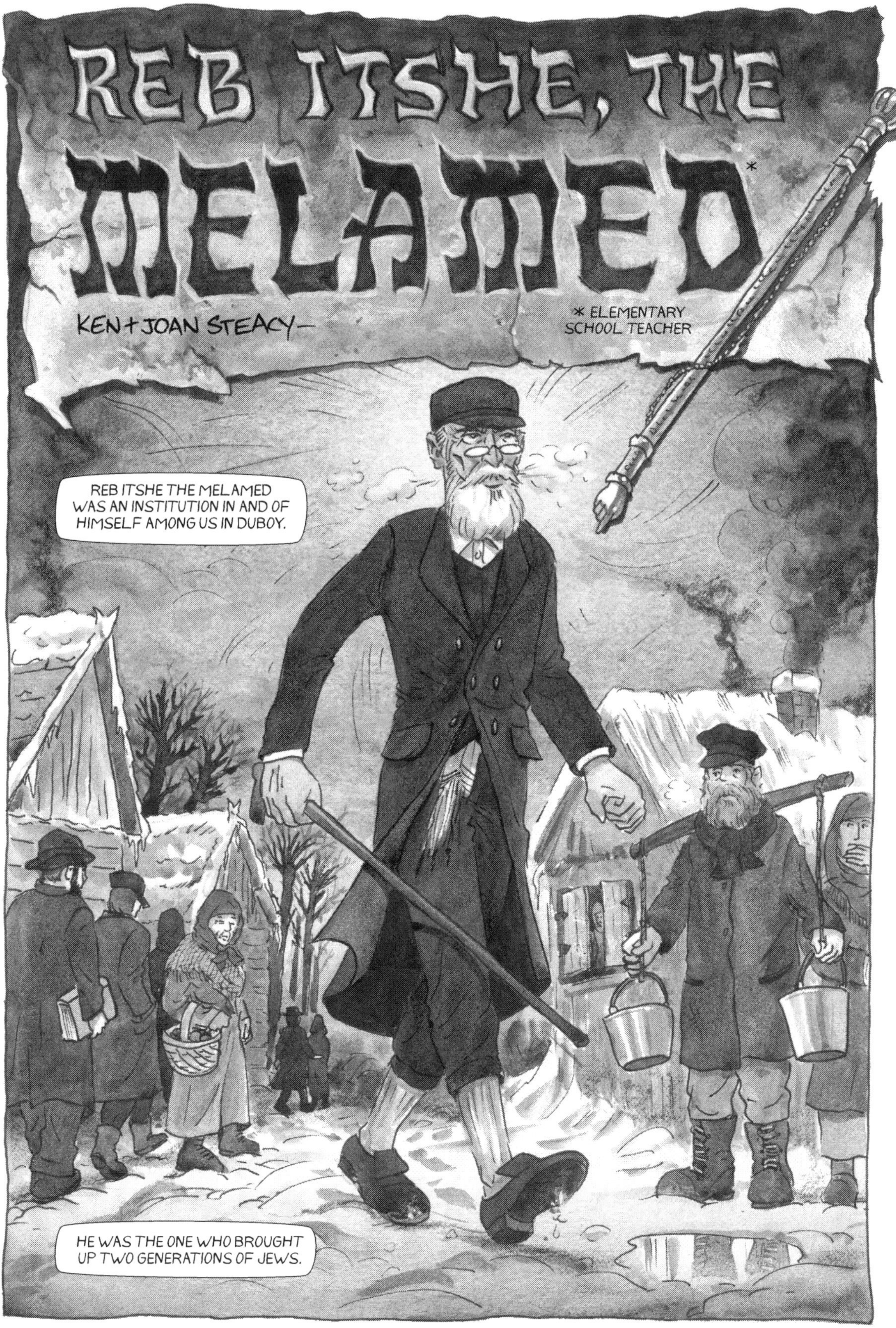
REB ITSHE, THE MELAMED*
KEN + JOAN STEACY
* ELEMENTARY SCHOOL TEACHER
REB ITSHE THE MELAMED WAS AN INSTITUTION IN AND OF HIMSELF AMONG US IN DUBOY.
HE WAS THE ONE WHO BROUGHT UP TWO GENERATIONS OF JEWS.

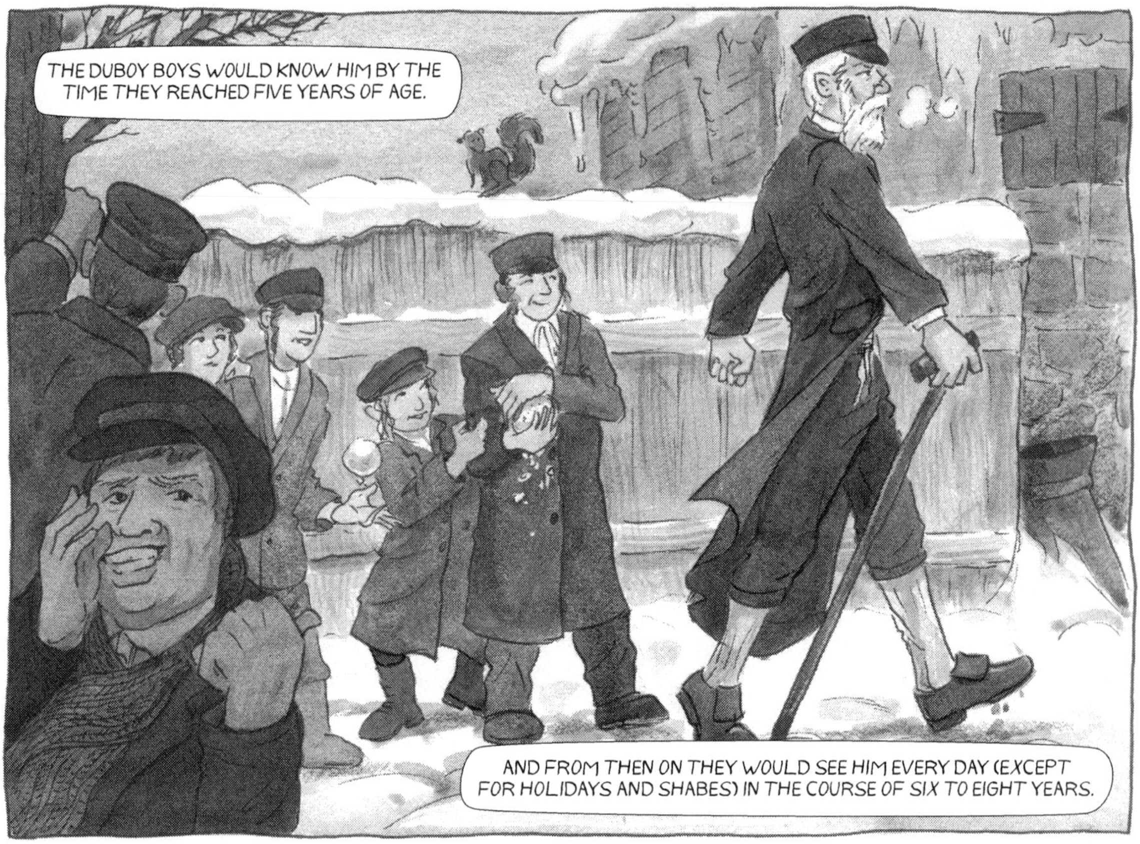
THE DUBOY BOYS WOULD KNOW HIM BY THE TIME THEY REACHED FIVE YEARS OF AGE.
AND FROM THEN ON THEY WOULD SEE HIM EVERY DAY (EXCEPT FOR HOLIDAYS AND SHABES) IN THE COURSE OF SIX TO EIGHT YEARS.

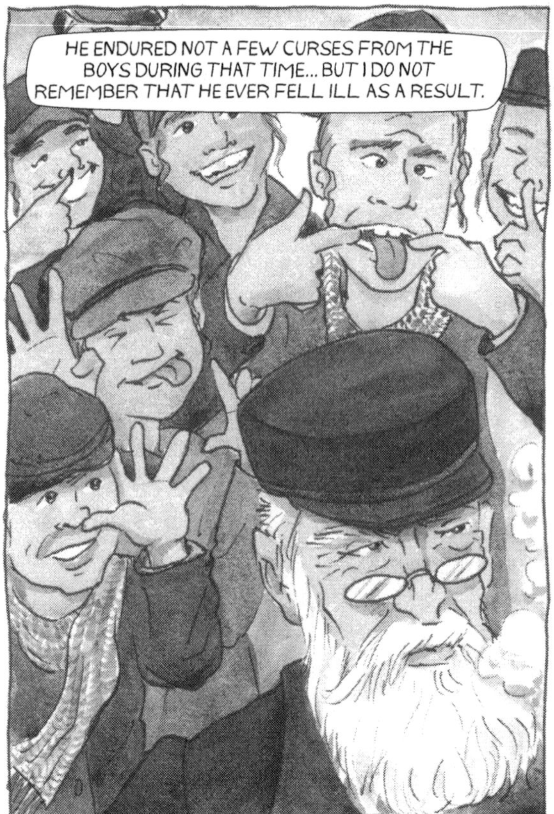
HE ENDURED NOT A FEW CURSES FROM THE BOYS DURING THAT TIME... BUT I DO NOT REMEMBER THAT HE EVER FELL ILL AS A RESULT.

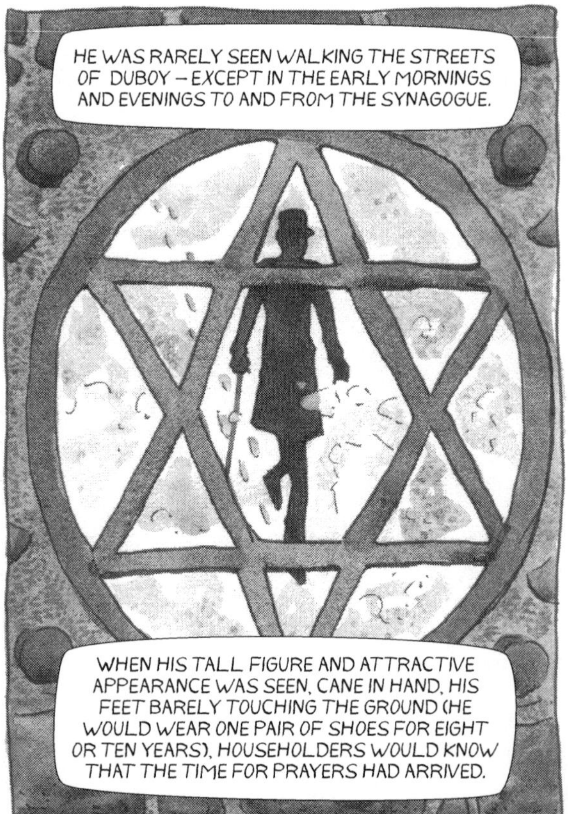
HE WAS RARELY SEEN WALKING THE STREETS OF DUBOY – EXCEPT IN THE EARLY MORNINGS AND EVENINGS TO AND FROM THE SYNAGOGUE.
WHEN HIS TALL FIGURE AND ATTRACTIVE APPEARANCE WAS SEEN, CANE IN HAND, HIS FEET BARELY TOUCHING THE GROUND (HE WOULD WEAR ONE PAIR OF SHOES FOR EIGHT OR TEN YEARS), HOUSEHOLDERS WOULD KNOW THAT THE TIME FOR PRAYERS HAD ARRIVED.

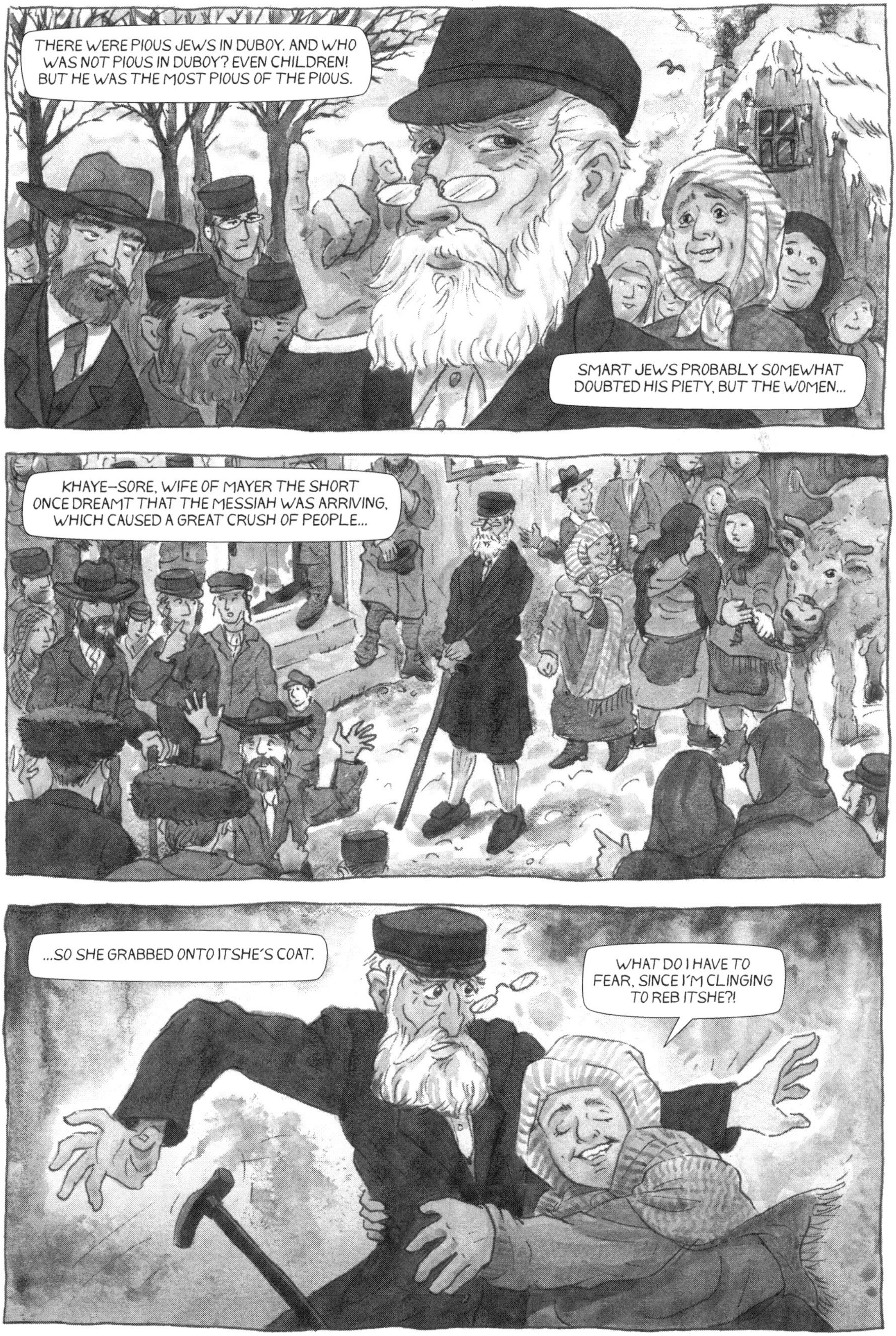
THERE WERE PIOUS JEWS IN DUBOY. AND WHO WAS NOT PIOUS IN DUBOY? EVEN CHILDREN! BUT HE WAS THE MOST PIOUS OF THE PIOUS.
SMART JEWS PROBABLY SOMEWHAT DOUBTED HIS PIETY, BUT THE WOMEN...
KHAYE-SORE, WIFE OF MAYER THE SHORT ONCE DREAMT THAT THE MESSIAH WAS ARRIVING, WHICH CAUSED A GREAT CRUSH OF PEOPLE...
...SO SHE GRABBED ONTO ITSHE'S COAT.
WHAT DO I HAVE TO FEAR, SINCE I'M CLINGING TO REB ITSHE?!

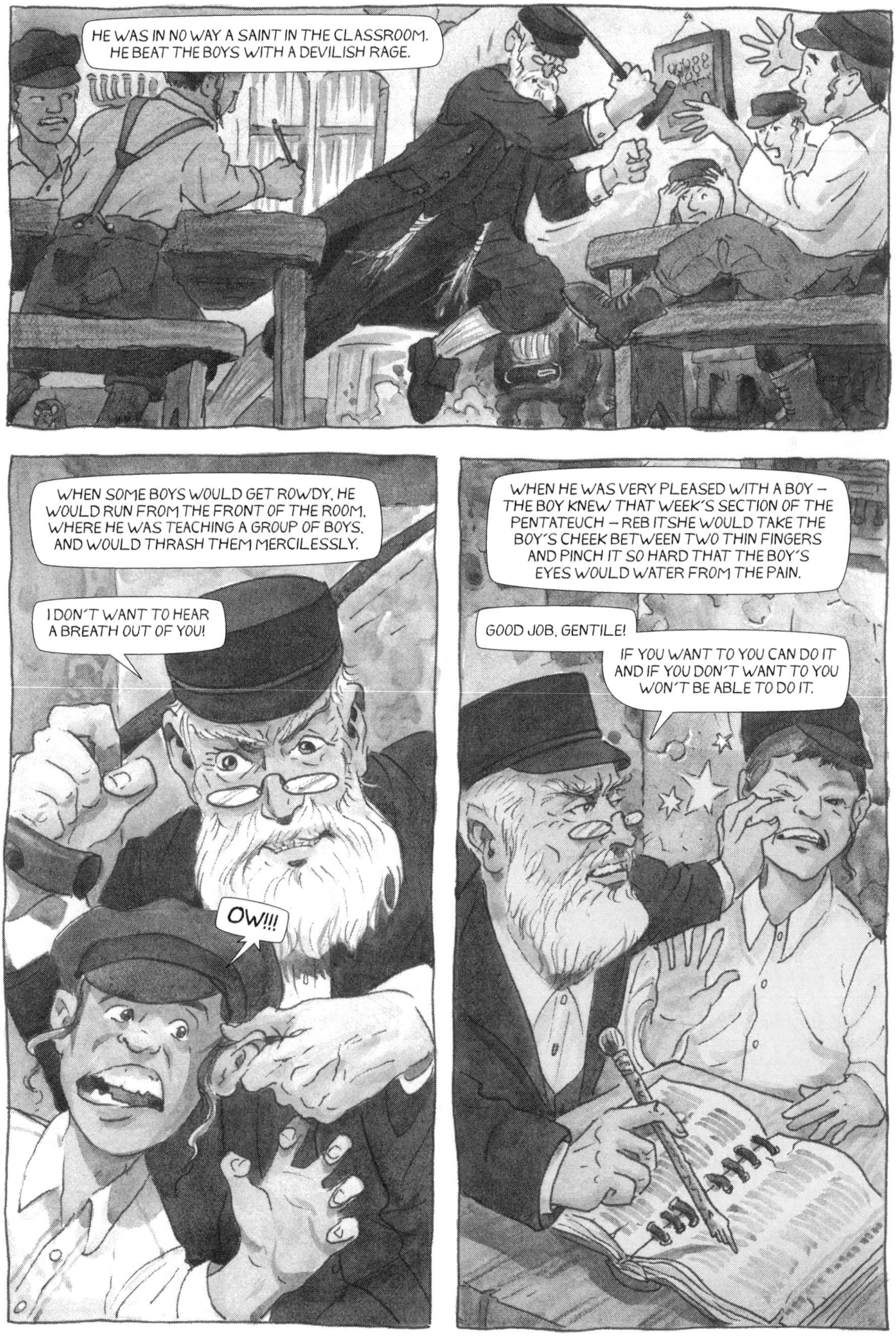
HE WAS IN NO WAY A SAINT IN THE CLASSROOM. HE BEAT THE BOYS WITH A DEVILISH RAGE.
WHEN SOME BOYS WOULD GET ROWDY, HE WOULD RUN FROM THE FRONT OF THE ROOM, WHERE HE WAS TEACHING A GROUP OF BOYS, AND WOULD THRASH THEM MERCILESSLY.
I DON'T WANT TO HEAR A BREATH OUT OF YOU!
OW!!!
WHEN HE WAS VERY PLEASED WITH A BOY – THE BOY KNEW THAT WEEK'S SECTION OF THE PENTATEUCH – REB ITSHE WOULD TAKE THE BOY'S CHEEK BETWEEN TWO THIN FINGERS AND PINCH IT SO HARD THAT THE BOY'S EYES WOULD WATER FROM THE PAIN.
GOOD JOB, GENTILE!
IF YOU WANT TO YOU CAN DO IT AND IF YOU DON'T WANT TO YOU WON'T BE ABLE TO DO IT.

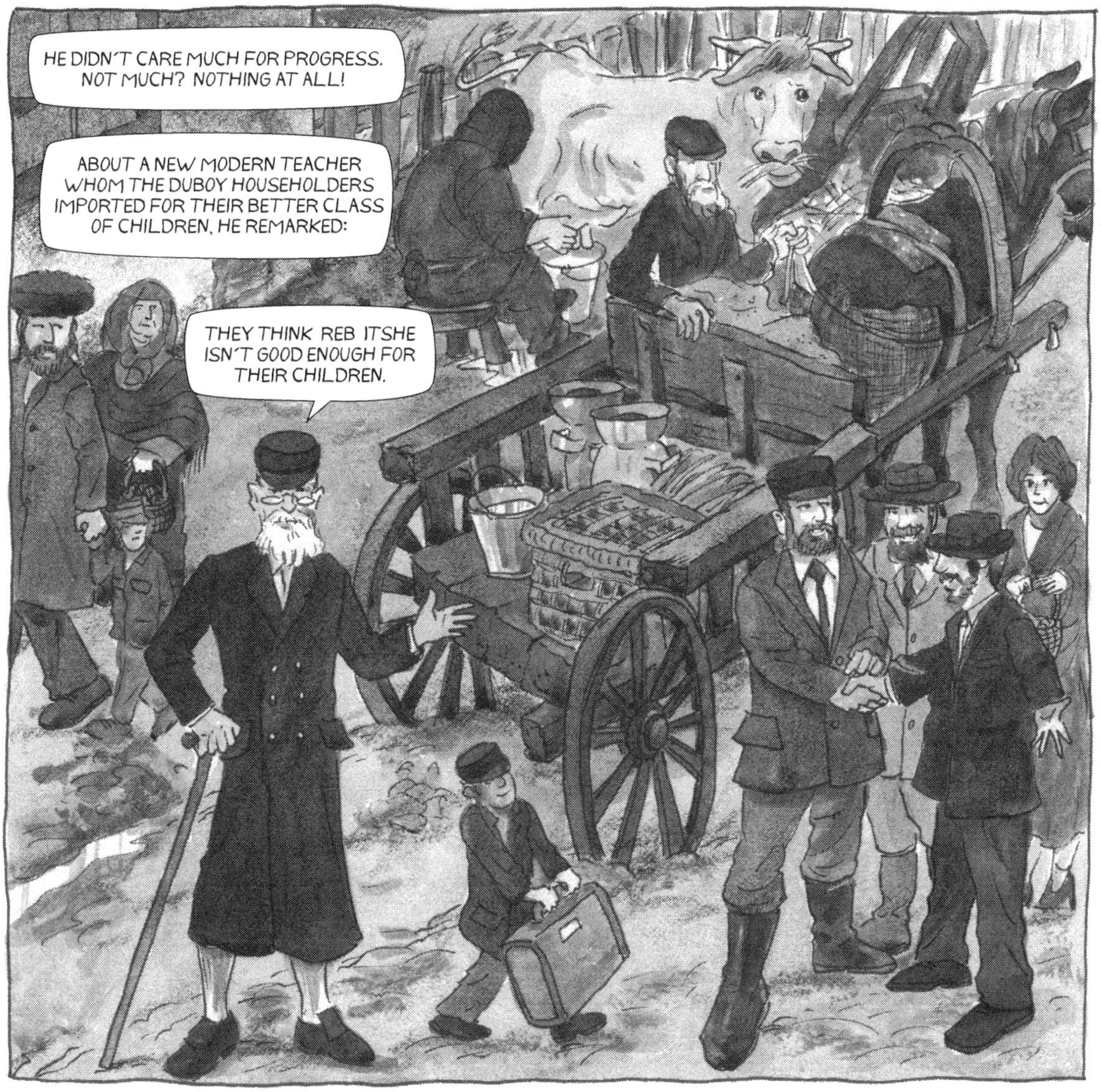
HE DIDN'T CARE MUCH FOR PROGRESS. NOT MUCH? NOTHING AT ALL!
ABOUT A NEW MODERN TEACHER WHOM THE DUBOY HOUSEHOLDERS IMPORTED FOR THEIR BETTER CLASS OF CHILDREN, HE REMARKED:
THEY THINK REB ITSHE ISN'T GOOD ENOUGH FOR THEIR CHILDREN.

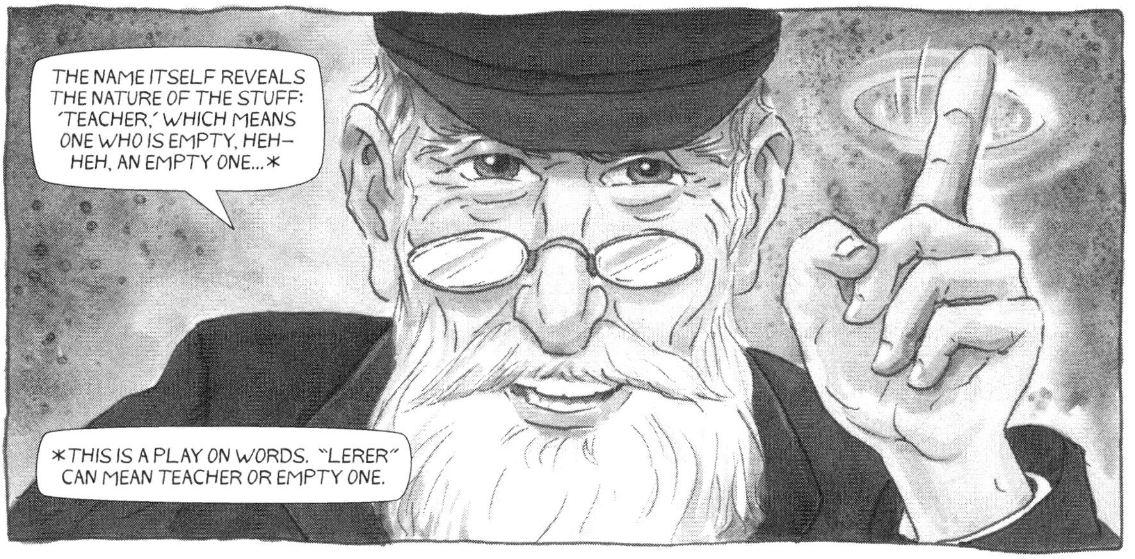
THE NAME ITSELF REVEALS THE NATURE OF THE STUFF: 'TEACHER,' WHICH MEANS ONE WHO IS EMPTY, HEH-HEH, AN EMPTY ONE...*
*THIS IS A PLAY ON WORDS. "LERER" CAN MEAN TEACHER OR EMPTY ONE.

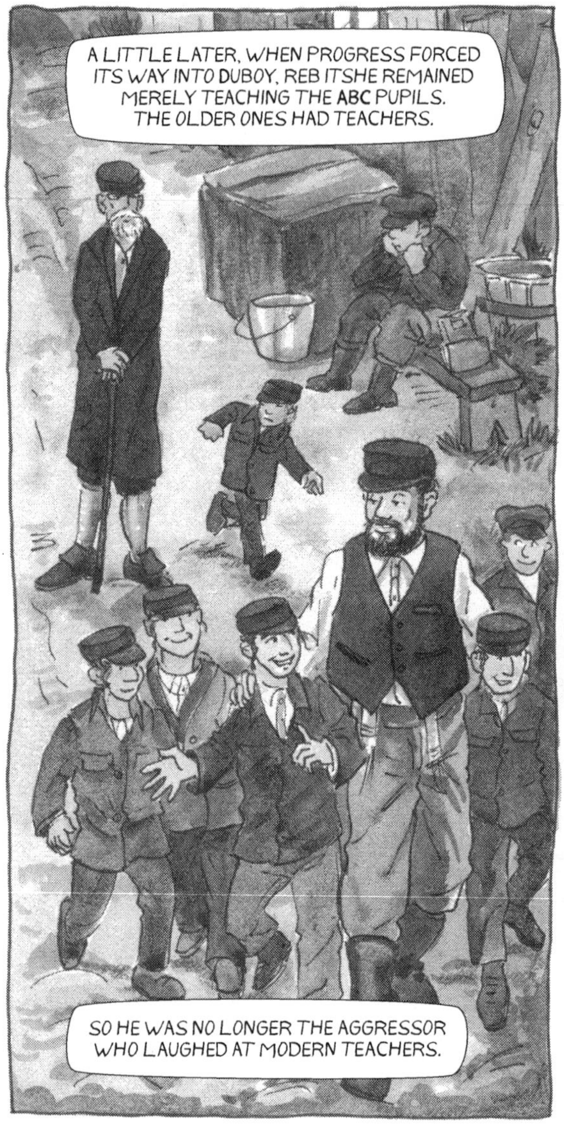
A LITTLE LATER, WHEN PROGRESS FORCED ITS WAY INTO DUBOY, REB ITSHE REMAINED MERELY TEACHING THE ABC PUPILS. THE OLDER ONES HAD TEACHERS.
SO HE WAS NO LONGER THE AGGRESSOR WHO LAUGHED AT MODERN TEACHERS.

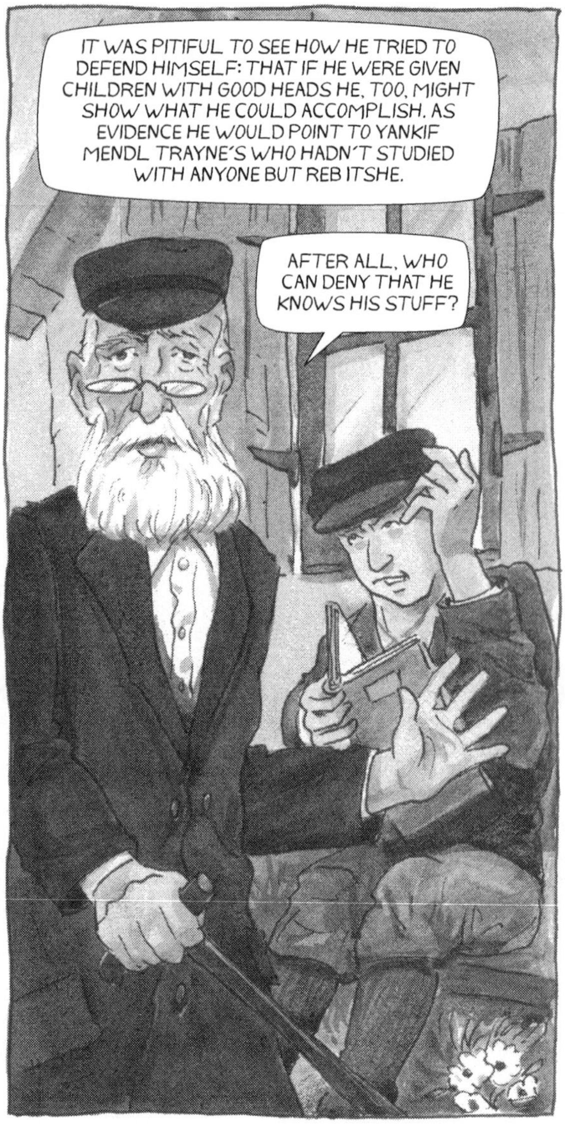
IT WAS PITIFUL TO SEE HOW HE TRIED TO DEFEND HIMSELF: THAT IF HE WERE GIVEN CHILDREN WITH GOOD HEADS HE, TOO, MIGHT SHOW WHAT HE COULD ACCOMPLISH. AS EVIDENCE HE WOULD POINT TO YANKIF MENDL TRAYNE'S WHO HADN'T STUDIED WITH ANYONE BUT REB ITSHE.
AFTER ALL, WHO CAN DENY THAT HE KNOWS HIS STUFF?

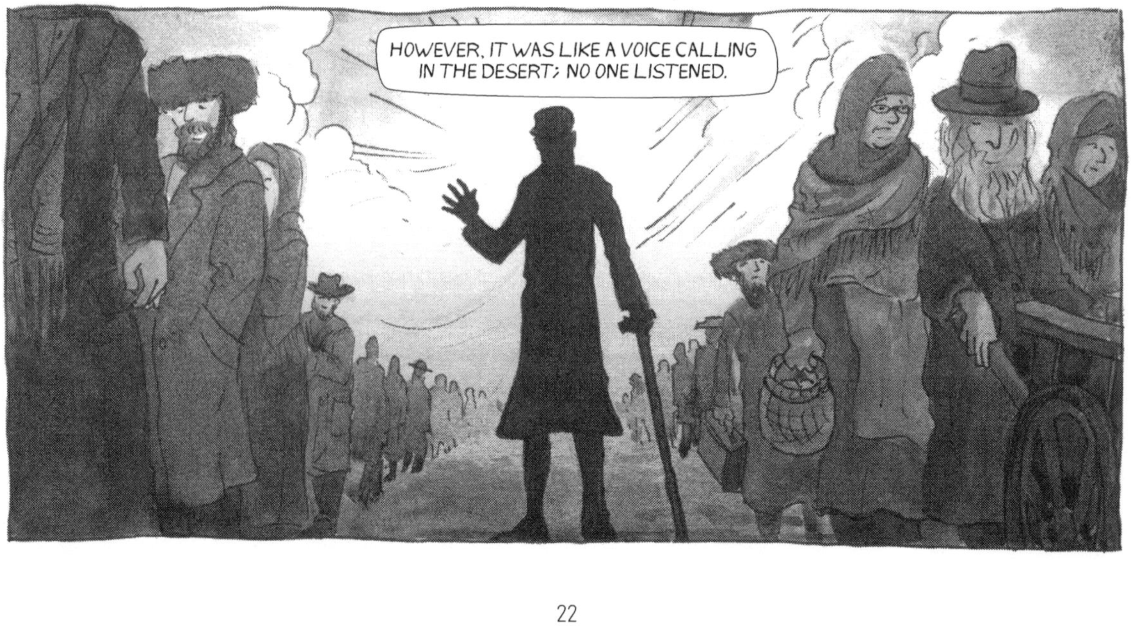
HOWEVER, IT WAS LIKE A VOICE CALLING IN THE DESERT; NO ONE LISTENED.

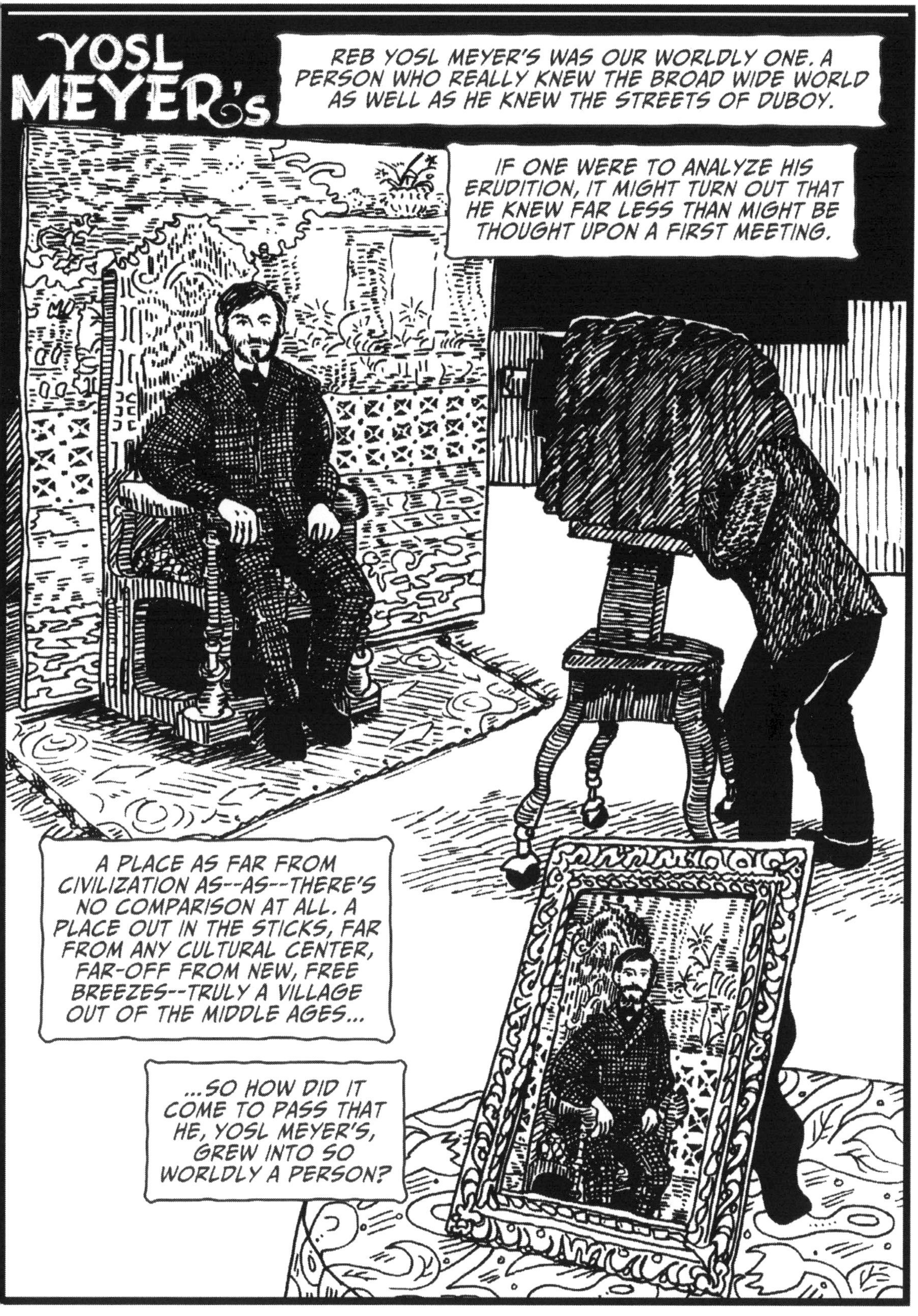
YOSL MEYER's
REB YOSL MEYER'S WAS OUR WORLDLY ONE. A PERSON WHO REALLY KNEW THE BROAD WIDE WORLD AS WELL AS HE KNEW THE STREETS OF DUBOY.
IF ONE WERE TO ANALYZE HIS ERUDITION, IT MIGHT TURN OUT THAT HE KNEW FAR LESS THAN MIGHT BE THOUGHT UPON A FIRST MEETING.
A PLACE AS FAR FROM CIVILIZATION AS--AS--THERE'S NO COMPARISON AT ALL. A PLACE OUT IN THE STICKS, FAR FROM ANY CULTURAL CENTER, FAR-OFF FROM NEW, FREE BREEZES--TRULY A VILLAGE OUT OF THE MIDDLE AGES...
...SO HOW DID IT COME TO PASS THAT HE, YOSL MEYER'S, GREW INTO SO WORLDLY A PERSON?

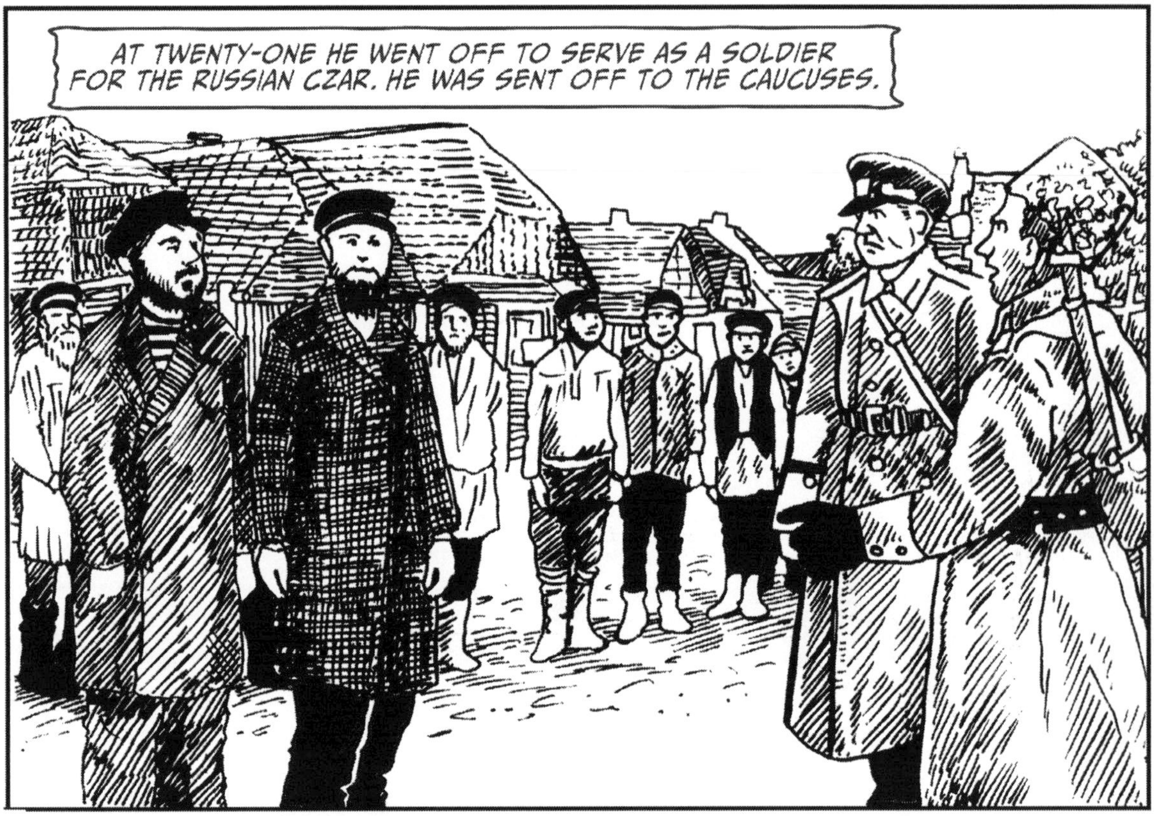
AT TWENTY-ONE HE WENT OFF TO SERVE AS A SOLDIER FOR THE RUSSIAN CZAR. HE WAS SENT OFF TO THE CAUCUSES.

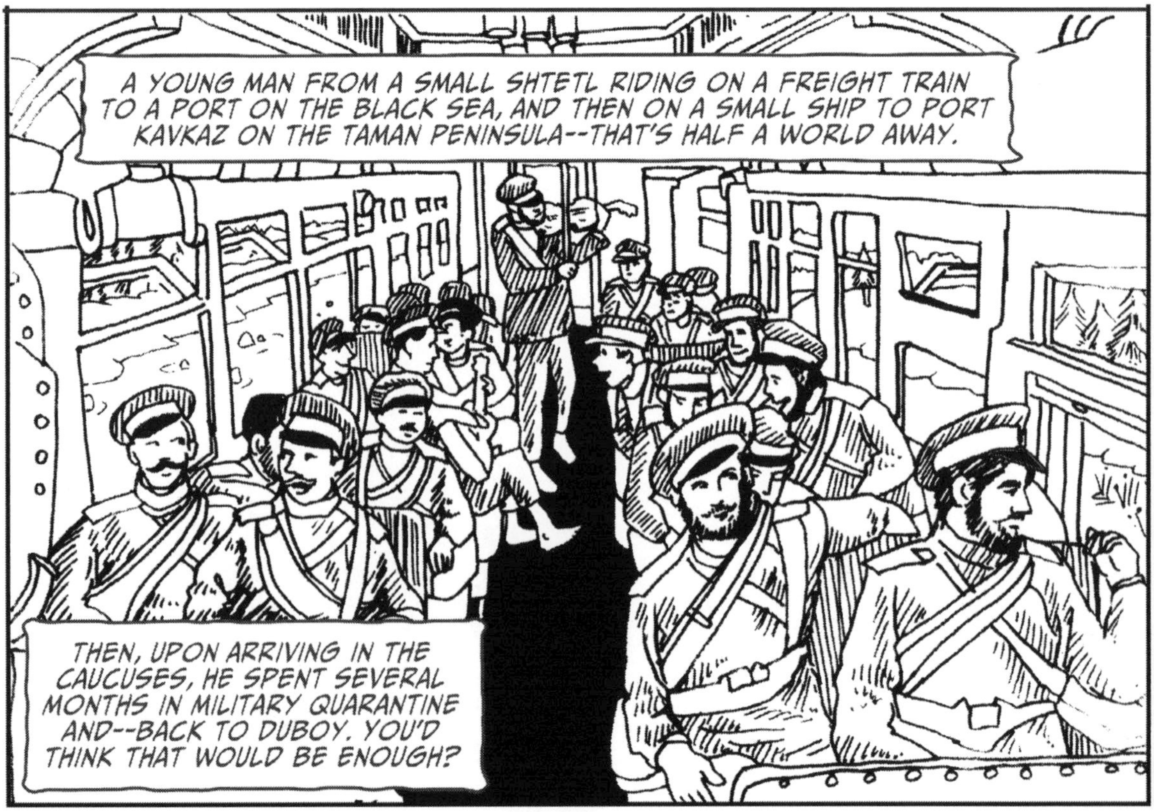
A YOUNG MAN FROM A SMALL SHTETL RIDING ON A FREIGHT TRAIN TO A PORT ON THE BLACK SEA, AND THEN ON A SMALL SHIP TO PORT KAVKAZ ON THE TAMAN PENINSULA--THAT'S HALF A WORLD AWAY.
THEN, UPON ARRIVING IN THE CAUCUSES, HE SPENT SEVERAL MONTHS IN MILITARY QUARANTINE AND--BACK TO DUBOY. YOU'D THINK THAT WOULD BE ENOUGH?

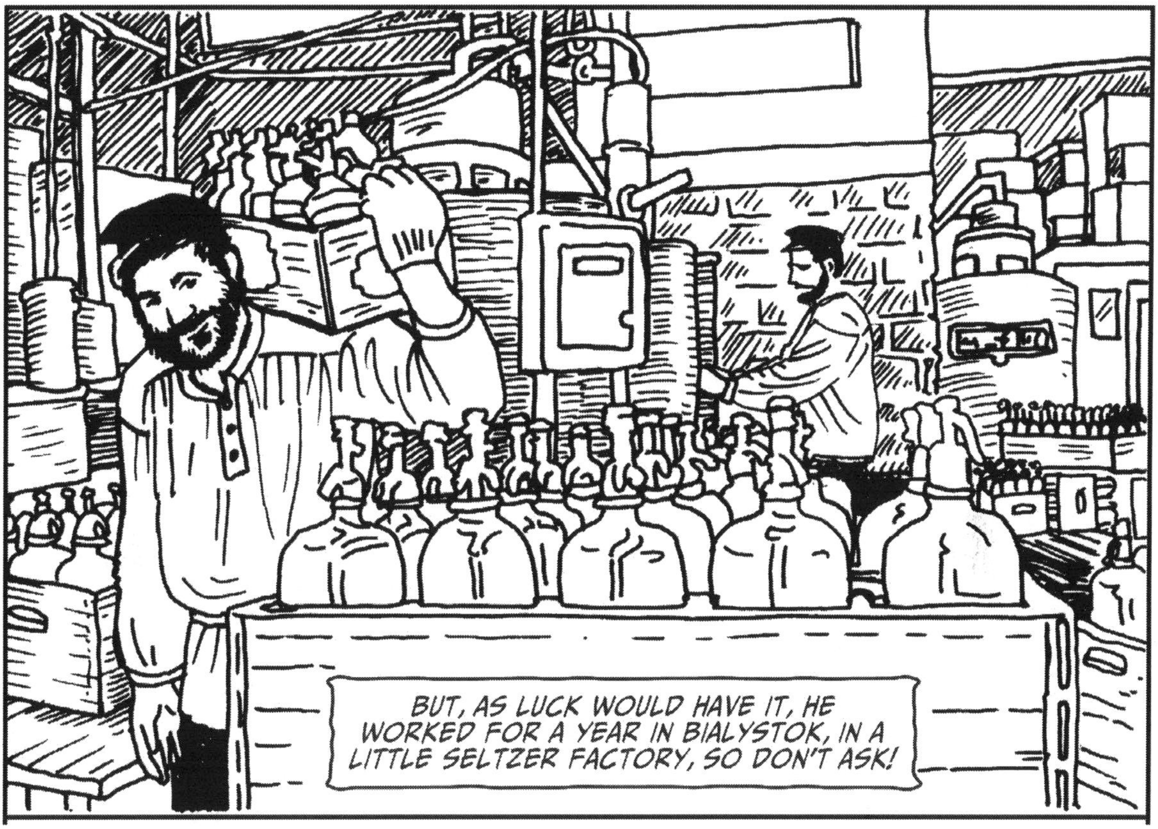
BUT, AS LUCK WOULD HAVE IT, HE WORKED FOR A YEAR IN BIALYSTOK, IN A LITTLE SELTZER FACTORY, SO DON'T ASK!

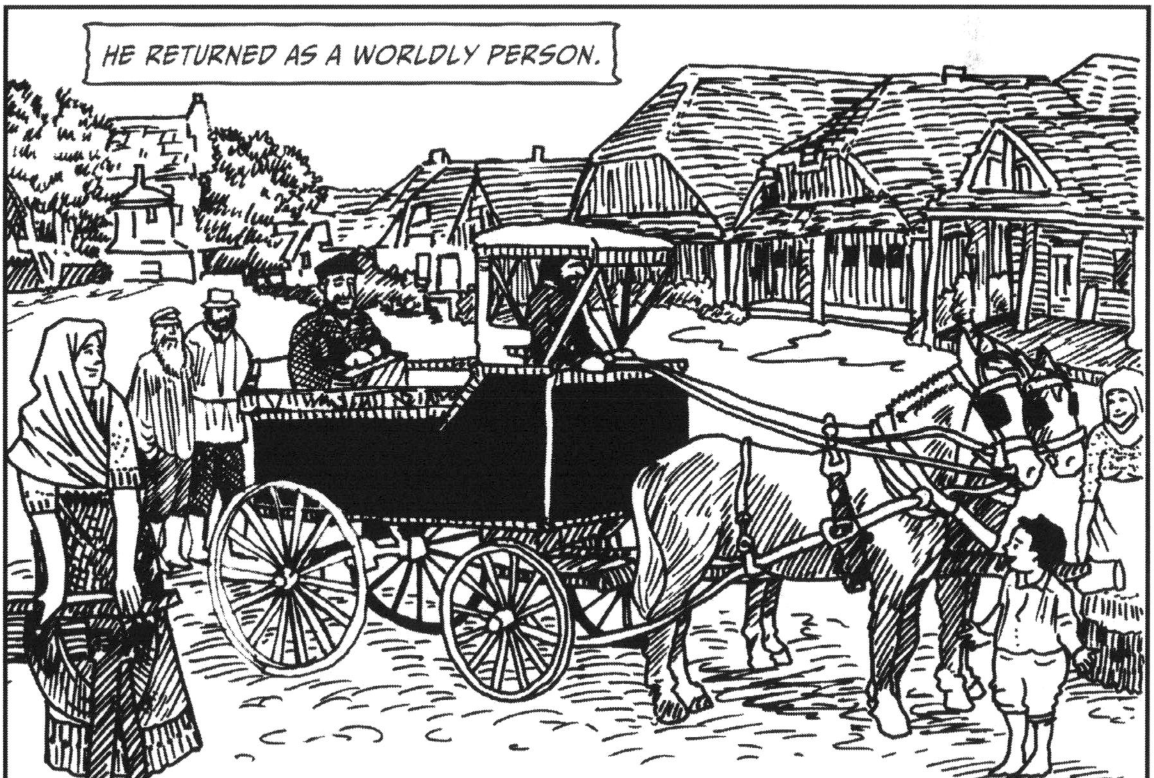
HE RETURNED AS A WORLDLY PERSON.

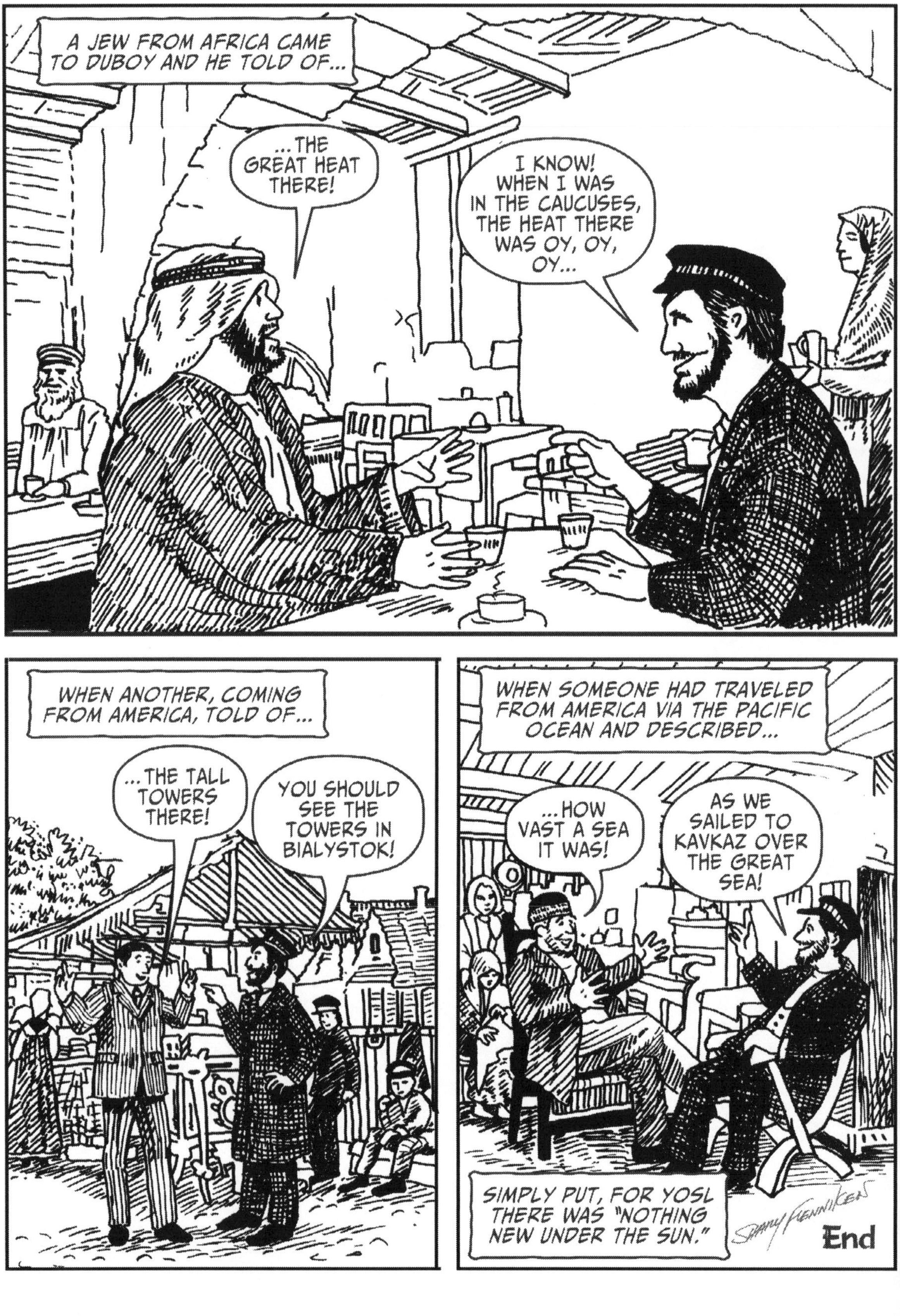
A JEW FROM AFRICA CAME TO DUBOY AND HE TOLD OF...
...THE GREAT HEAT THERE!
I KNOW! WHEN I WAS IN THE CAUCUSES, THE HEAT THERE WAS OY, OY, OY...
WHEN ANOTHER, COMING FROM AMERICA, TOLD OF...
...THE TALL TOWERS THERE!
YOU SHOULD SEE THE TOWERS IN BIALYSTOK!
WHEN SOMEONE HAD TRAVELED FROM AMERICA VIA THE PACIFIC OCEAN AND DESCRIBED...
...HOW VAST A SEA IT WAS!
AS WE SAILED TO KAVKAZ OVER THE GREAT SEA!
SIMPLY PUT, FOR YOSL THERE WAS "NOTHING NEW UNDER THE SUN."
End

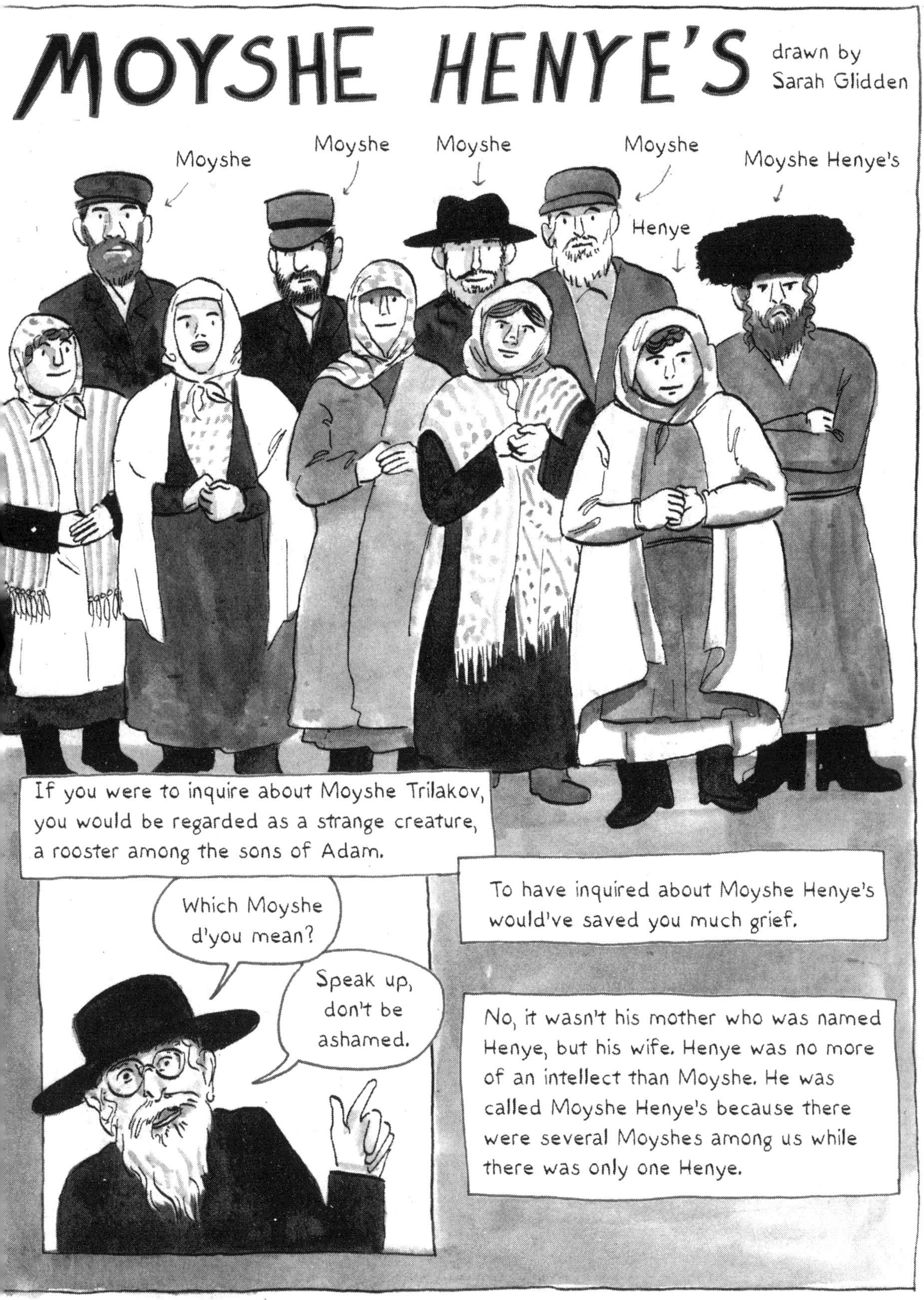

MOYSHE HENYE'S
drawn by
Sarah Glidden
Moyshe
Moyshe
Moyshe
Moyshe
Henye
Moyshe Henye's
If you were to inquire about Moyshe Trilakov, you would be regarded as a strange creature, a rooster among the sons of Adam.
Which Moyshe d'you mean?
Speak up, don't be ashamed.
To have inquired about Moyshe Henye's would've saved you much grief.
No, it wasn't his mother who was named Henye, but his wife. Henye was no more of an intellect than Moyshe. He was called Moyshe Henye's because there were several Moyshes among us while there was only one Henye.

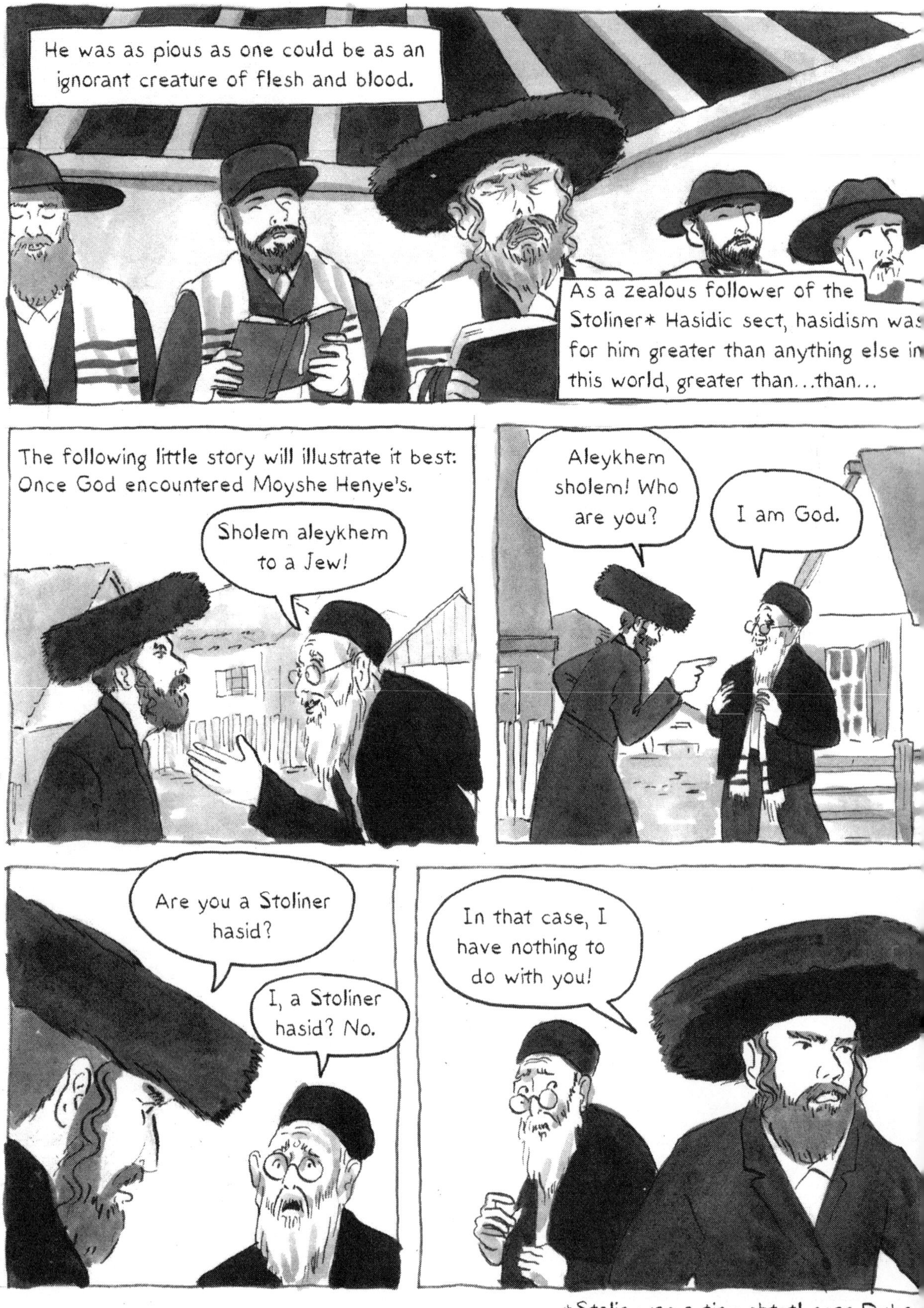
He was as pious as one could be as an ignorant creature of flesh and blood.
As a zealous follower of the Stoliner* Hasidic sect, hasidism was for him greater than anything else in this world, greater than...than...
The following little story will illustrate it best: Once God encountered Moyshe Henye's.
Sholem aleykhem to a Jew!
Aleykhem sholem! Who are you?
I am God.
Are you a Stoliner hasid?
I, a Stoliner hasid? No.
In that case, I have nothing to do with you!

*Stolin was a tiny shtetl near Duboy

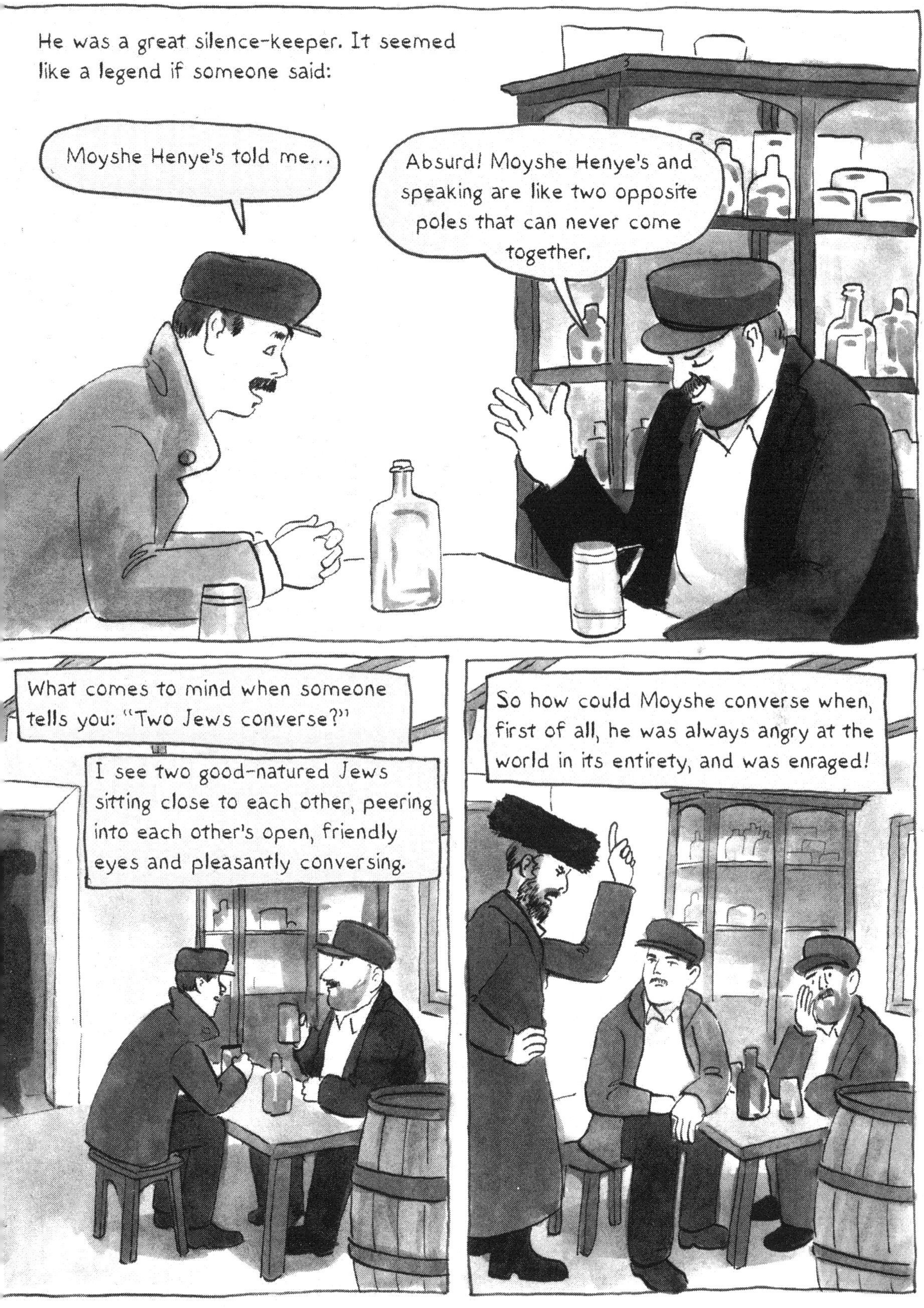
He was a great silence-keeper. It seemed like a legend if someone said:
Moyshe Henye's told me...
Absurd! Moyshe Henye's and speaking are like two opposite poles that can never come together.
What comes to mind when someone tells you: "Two Jews converse?"
I see two good-natured Jews sitting close to each other, peering into each other's open, friendly eyes and pleasantly conversing.
So how could Moyshe converse when, first of all, he was always angry at the world in its entirety, and was enraged!

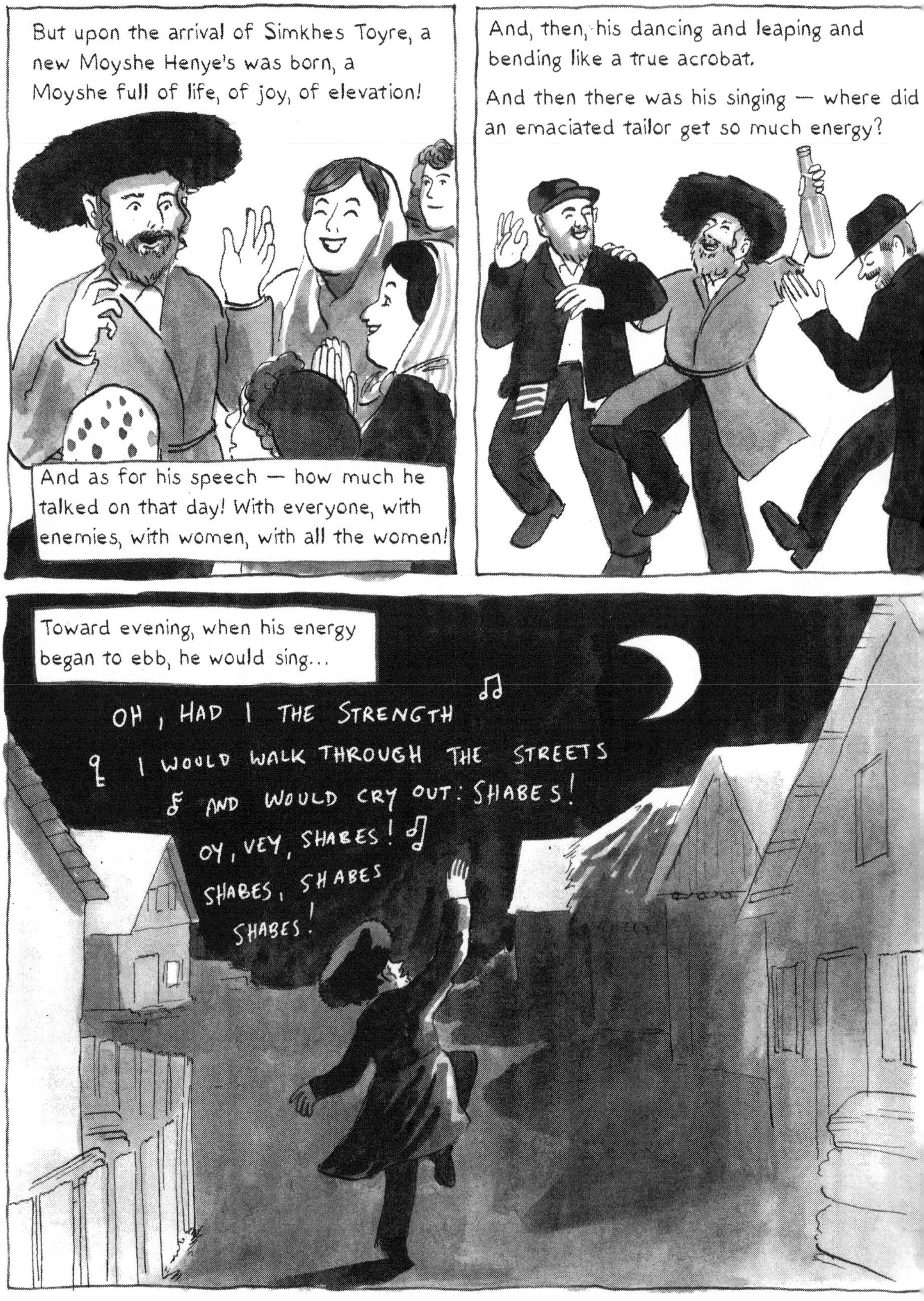
But upon the arrival of Simkhes Toyre, a new Moyshe Henye's was born, a Moyshe full of life, of joy, of elevation!
And as for his speech — how much he talked on that day! With everyone, with enemies, with women, with all the women!
And, then, his dancing and leaping and bending like a true acrobat.
And then there was his singing — where did an emaciated tailor get so much energy?
Toward evening, when his energy began to ebb, he would sing...
OH, HAD I THE STRENGTH
I WOULD WALK THROUGH THE STREETS
AND WOULD CRY OUT: SHABES!
OY, VEY, SHABES!
SHABES, SHABES
SHABES!

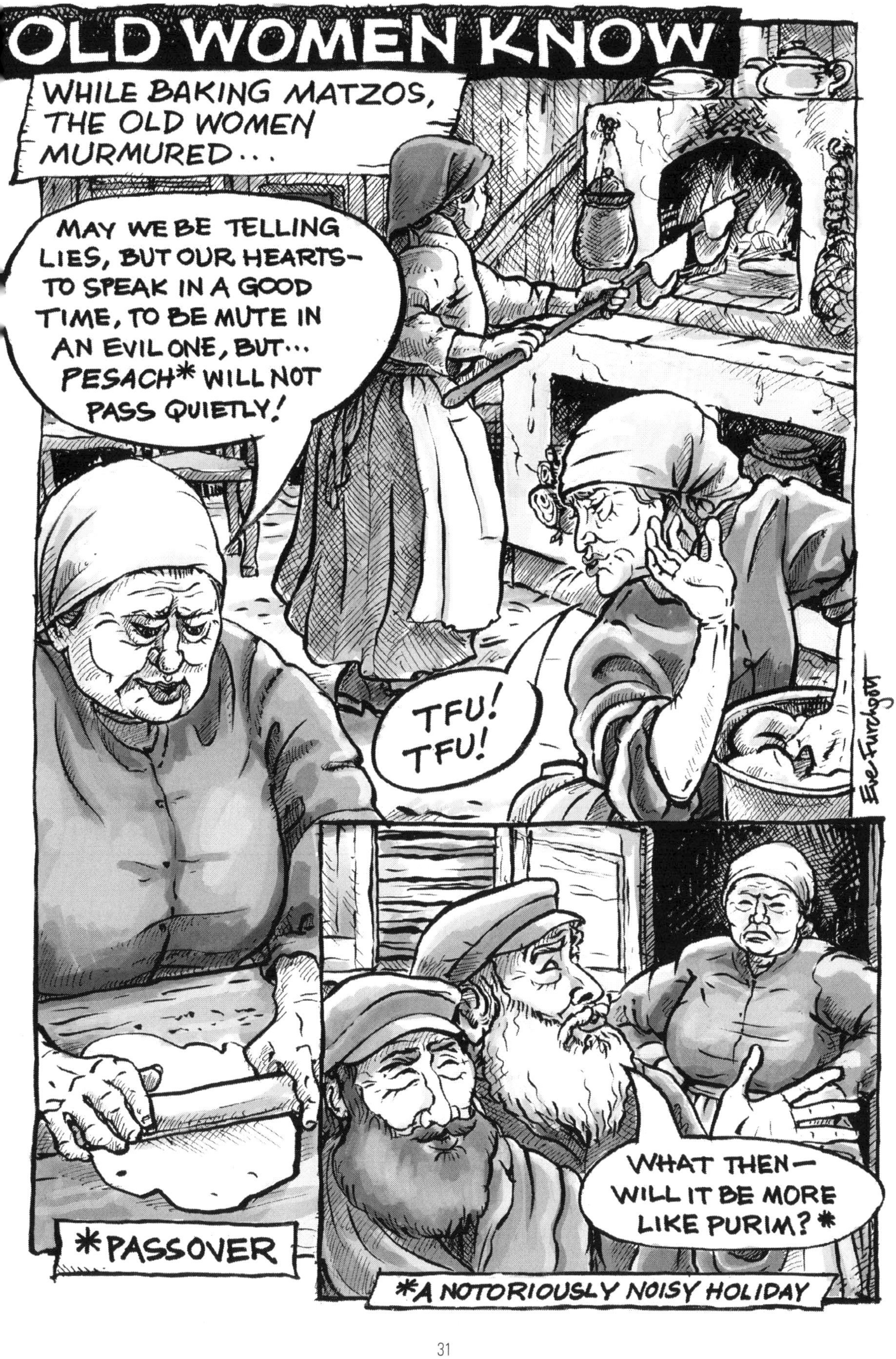
OLD WOMEN KNOW
WHILE BAKING MATZOS, THE OLD WOMEN MURMURED...
MAY WE BE TELLING LIES, BUT OUR HEARTS- TO SPEAK IN A GOOD TIME, TO BE MUTE IN AN EVIL ONE, BUT... PESACH* WILL NOT PASS QUIETLY!
TFU! TFU!
Eve Furchgott
*PASSOVER
WHAT THEN- WILL IT BE MORE LIKE PURIM?*
*A NOTORIOUSLY NOISY HOLIDAY

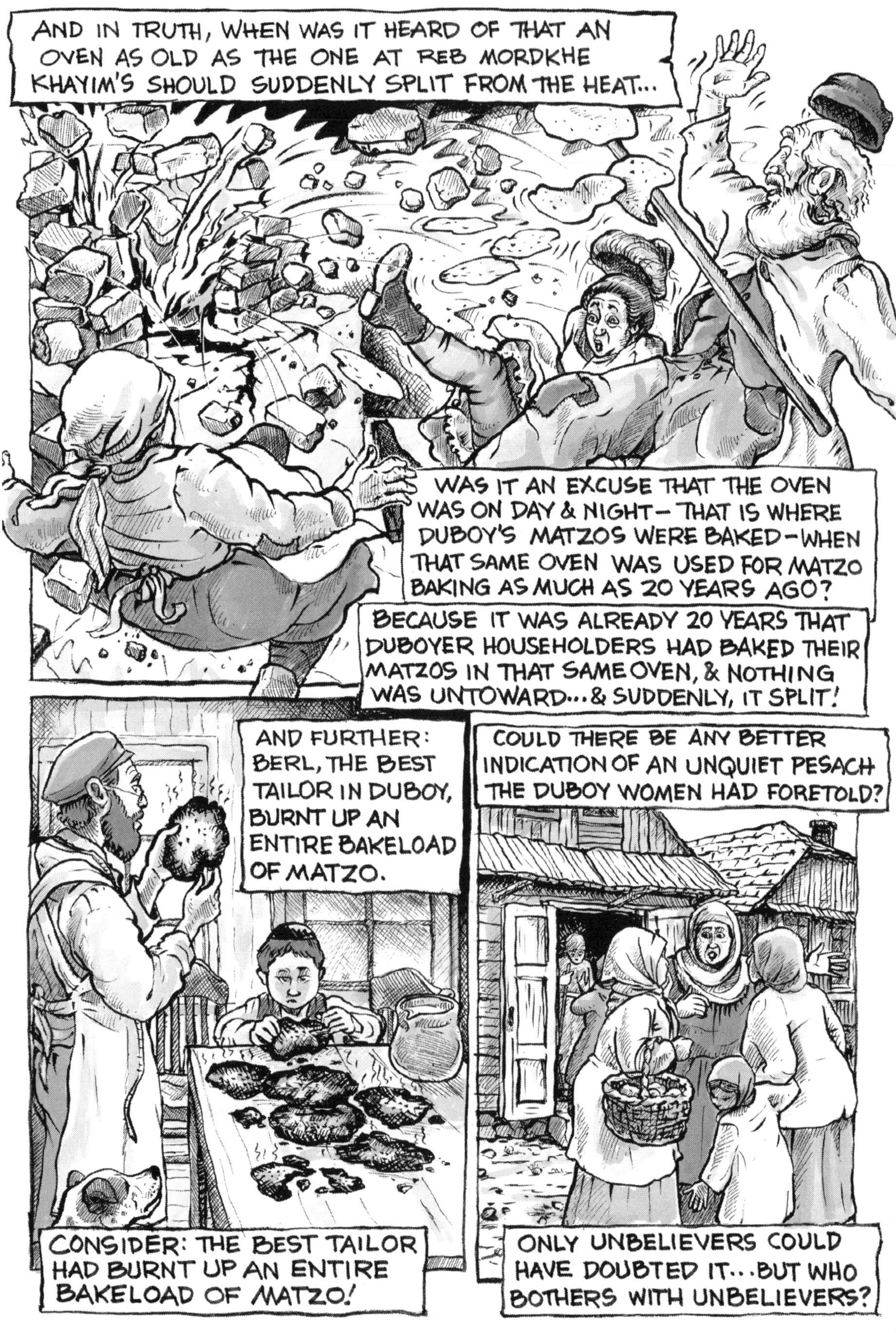
AND IN TRUTH, WHEN WAS IT HEARD OF THAT AN OVEN AS OLD AS THE ONE AT REB MORDKHE KHAYIM'S SHOULD SUDDENLY SPLIT FROM THE HEAT...
WAS IT AN EXCUSE THAT THE OVEN WAS ON DAY & NIGHT – THAT IS WHERE DUBOY'S MATZOS WERE BAKED – WHEN THAT SAME OVEN WAS USED FOR MATZO BAKING AS MUCH AS 20 YEARS AGO?
BECAUSE IT WAS ALREADY 20 YEARS THAT DUBOYER HOUSEHOLDERS HAD BAKED THEIR MATZOS IN THAT SAME OVEN, & NOTHING WAS UNTOWARD... & SUDDENLY, IT SPLIT!
AND FURTHER: BERL, THE BEST TAILOR IN DUBOY, BURNT UP AN ENTIRE BAKELOAD OF MATZO.
CONSIDER: THE BEST TAILOR HAD BURNT UP AN ENTIRE BAKELOAD OF MATZO!
COULD THERE BE ANY BETTER INDICATION OF AN UNQUIET PESACH THE DUBOY WOMEN HAD FORETOLD?
ONLY UNBELIEVERS COULD HAVE DOUBTED IT... BUT WHO BOTHERS WITH UNBELIEVERS?

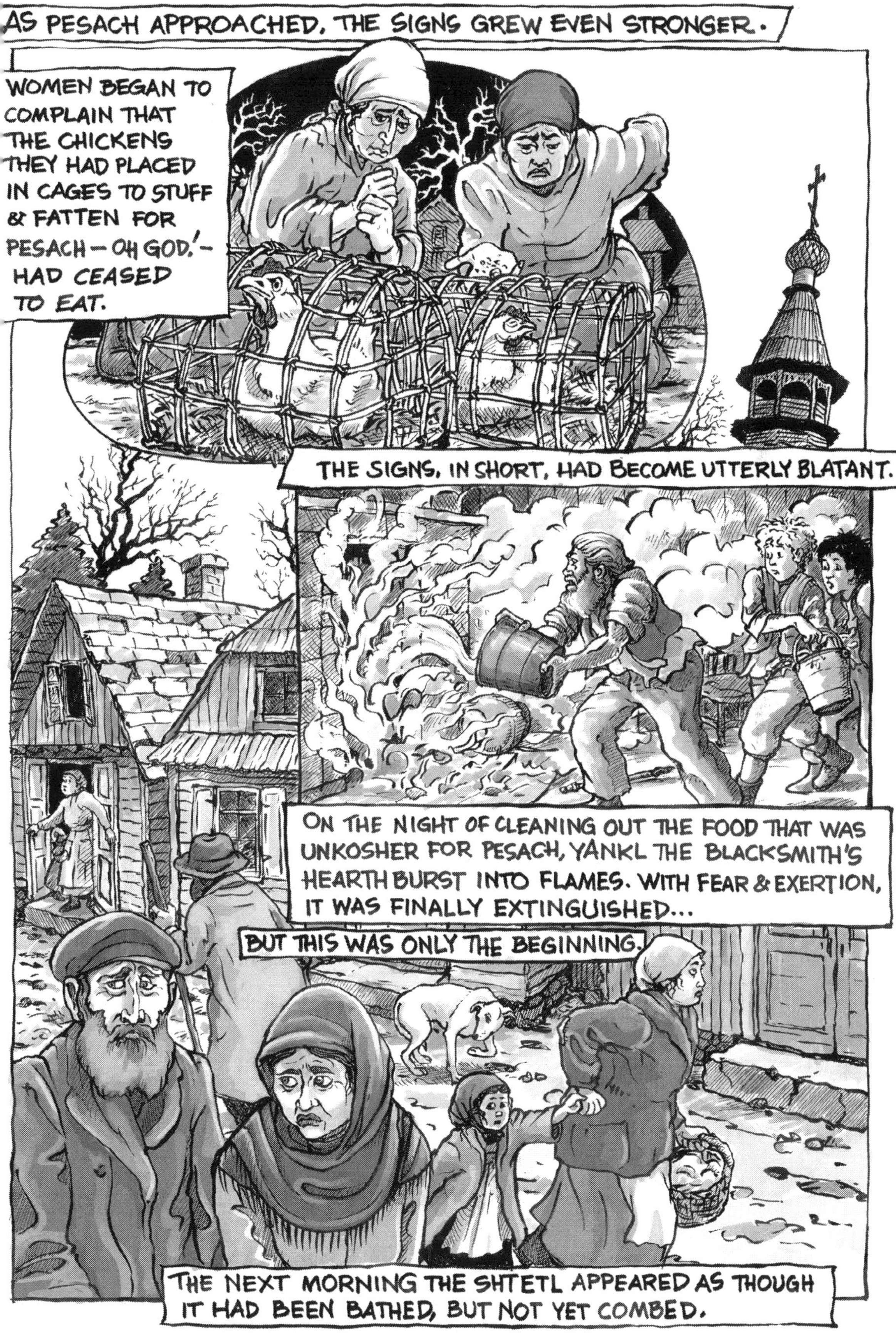
AS PESACH APPROACHED, THE SIGNS GREW EVEN STRONGER.
WOMEN BEGAN TO COMPLAIN THAT THE CHICKENS THEY HAD PLACED IN CAGES TO STUFF & FATTEN FOR PESACH — OH GOD! — HAD CEASED TO EAT.
THE SIGNS, IN SHORT, HAD BECOME UTTERLY BLATANT.
ON THE NIGHT OF CLEANING OUT THE FOOD THAT WAS UNKOSHER FOR PESACH, YANKL THE BLACKSMITH'S HEARTH BURST INTO FLAMES. WITH FEAR & EXERTION, IT WAS FINALLY EXTINGUISHED...
BUT THIS WAS ONLY THE BEGINNING.
THE NEXT MORNING THE SHTETL APPEARED AS THOUGH IT HAD BEEN BATHED, BUT NOT YET COMBED.

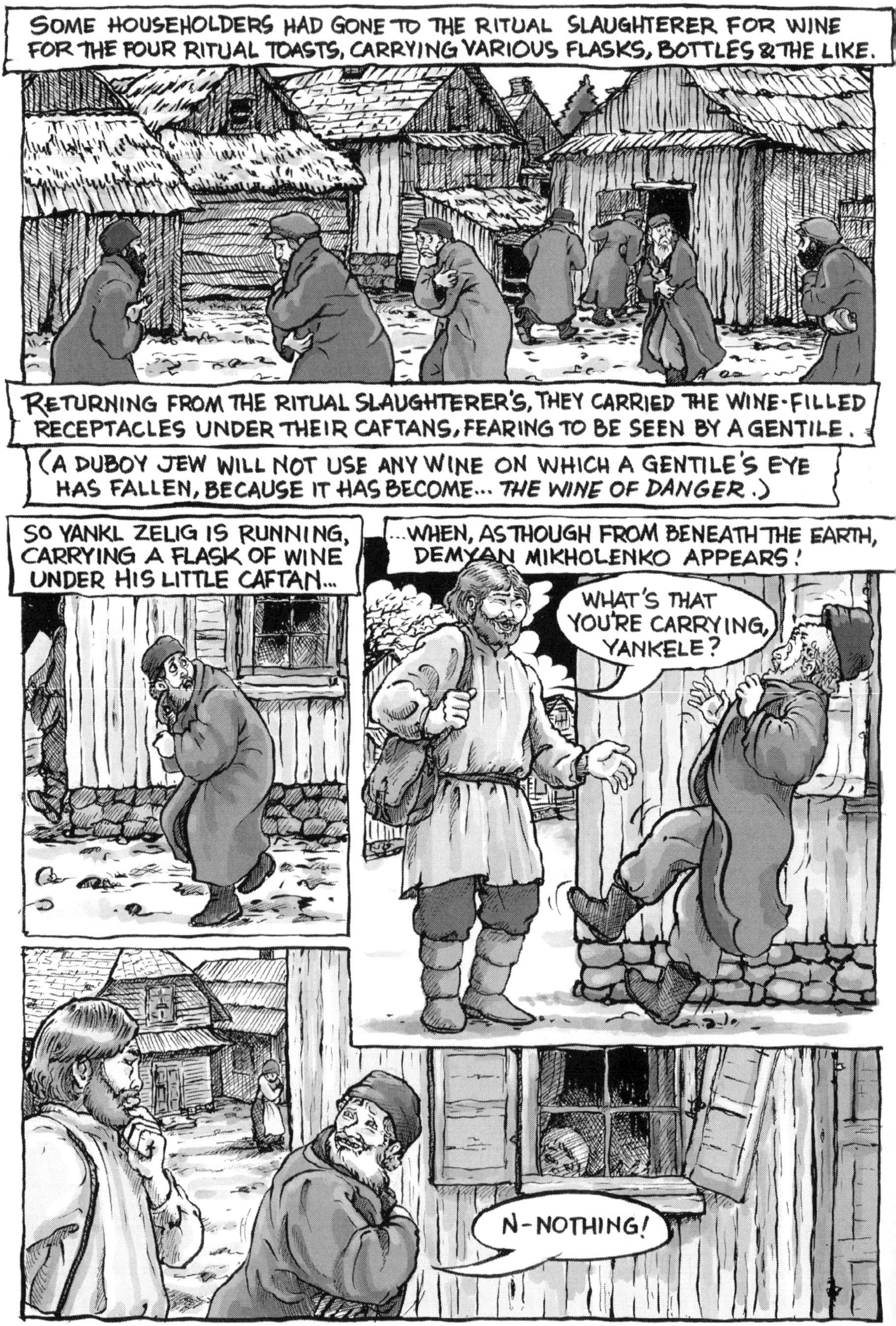
SOME HOUSEHOLDERS HAD GONE TO THE RITUAL SLAUGHTERER FOR WINE FOR THE FOUR RITUAL TOASTS, CARRYING VARIOUS FLASKS, BOTTLES & THE LIKE.
RETURNING FROM THE RITUAL SLAUGHTERER'S, THEY CARRIED THE WINE-FILLED RECEPTACLES UNDER THEIR CAFTANS, FEARING TO BE SEEN BY A GENTILE.
(A DUBOY JEW WILL NOT USE ANY WINE ON WHICH A GENTILE'S EYE HAS FALLEN, BECAUSE IT HAS BECOME... *THE WINE OF DANGER*.)
SO YANKL ZELIG IS RUNNING, CARRYING A FLASK OF WINE UNDER HIS LITTLE CAFTAN...
...WHEN, AS THOUGH FROM BENEATH THE EARTH, DEMYAN MIKHOLENKO APPEARS!
WHAT'S THAT YOU'RE CARRYING, YANKELE?
N-NOTHING!

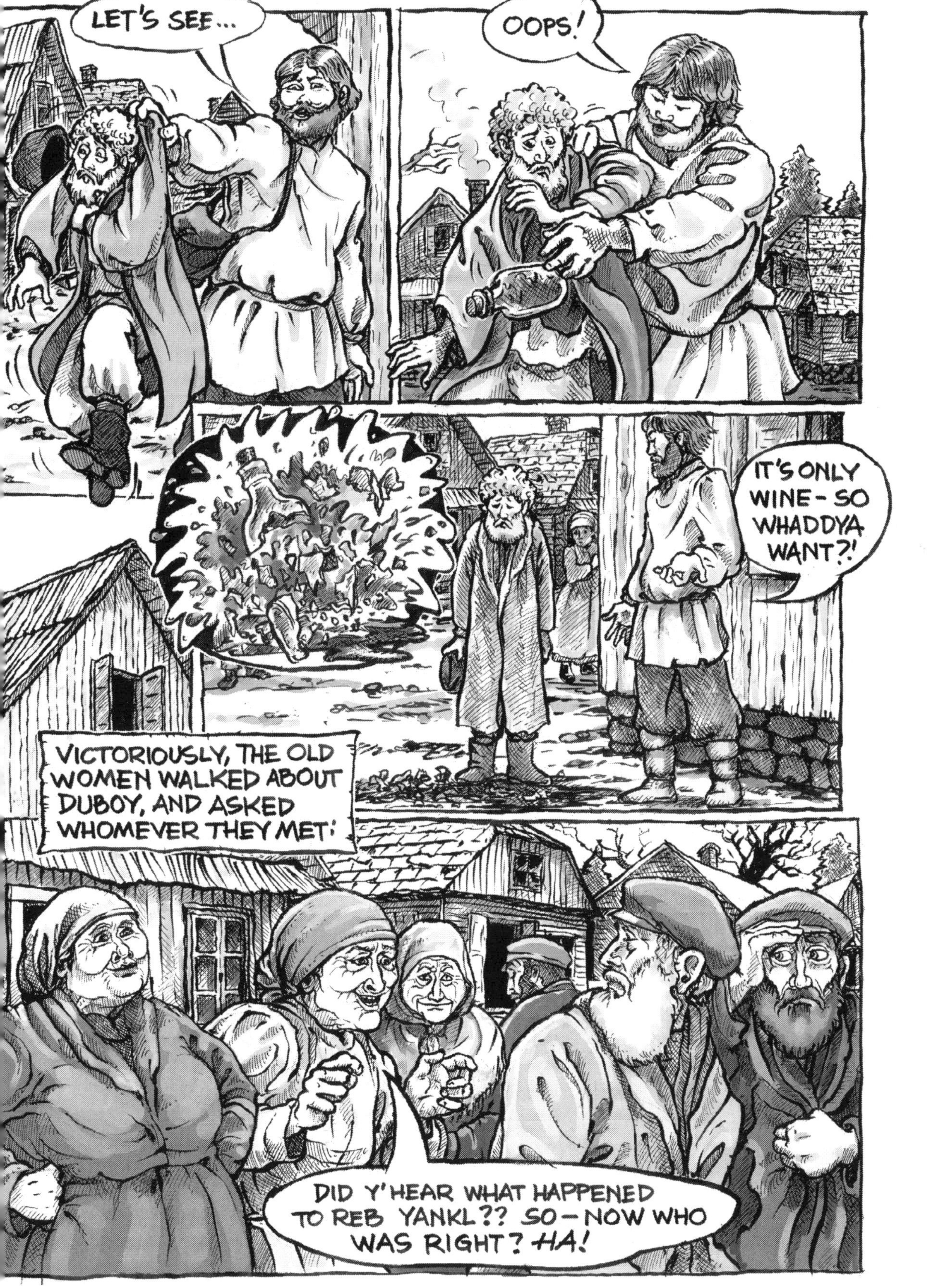
LET'S SEE...
OOPS!
IT'S ONLY WINE- SO WHADDYA WANT?!
VICTORIOUSLY, THE OLD WOMEN WALKED ABOUT DUBOY, AND ASKED WHOMEVER THEY MET:
DID Y' HEAR WHAT HAPPENED TO REB YANKL?? SO- NOW WHO WAS RIGHT? HA!

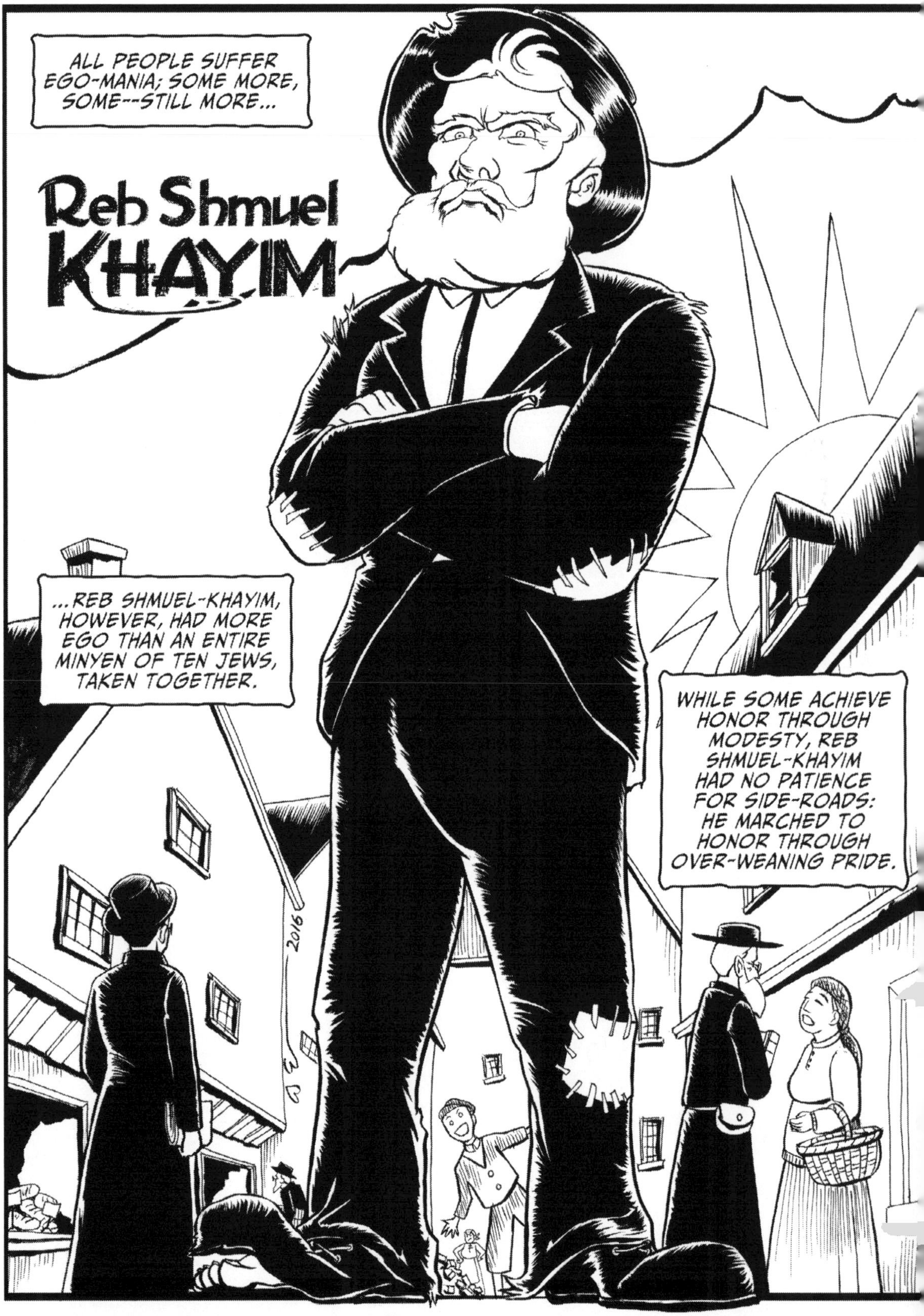
ALL PEOPLE SUFFER EGO-MANIA; SOME MORE, SOME--STILL MORE...
Reb Shmuel KHAYIM
...REB SHMUEL-KHAYIM, HOWEVER, HAD MORE EGO THAN AN ENTIRE MINYEN OF TEN JEWS, TAKEN TOGETHER.
WHILE SOME ACHIEVE HONOR THROUGH MODESTY, REB SHMUEL-KHAYIM HAD NO PATIENCE FOR SIDE-ROADS: HE MARCHED TO HONOR THROUGH OVER-WEANING PRIDE.
2016

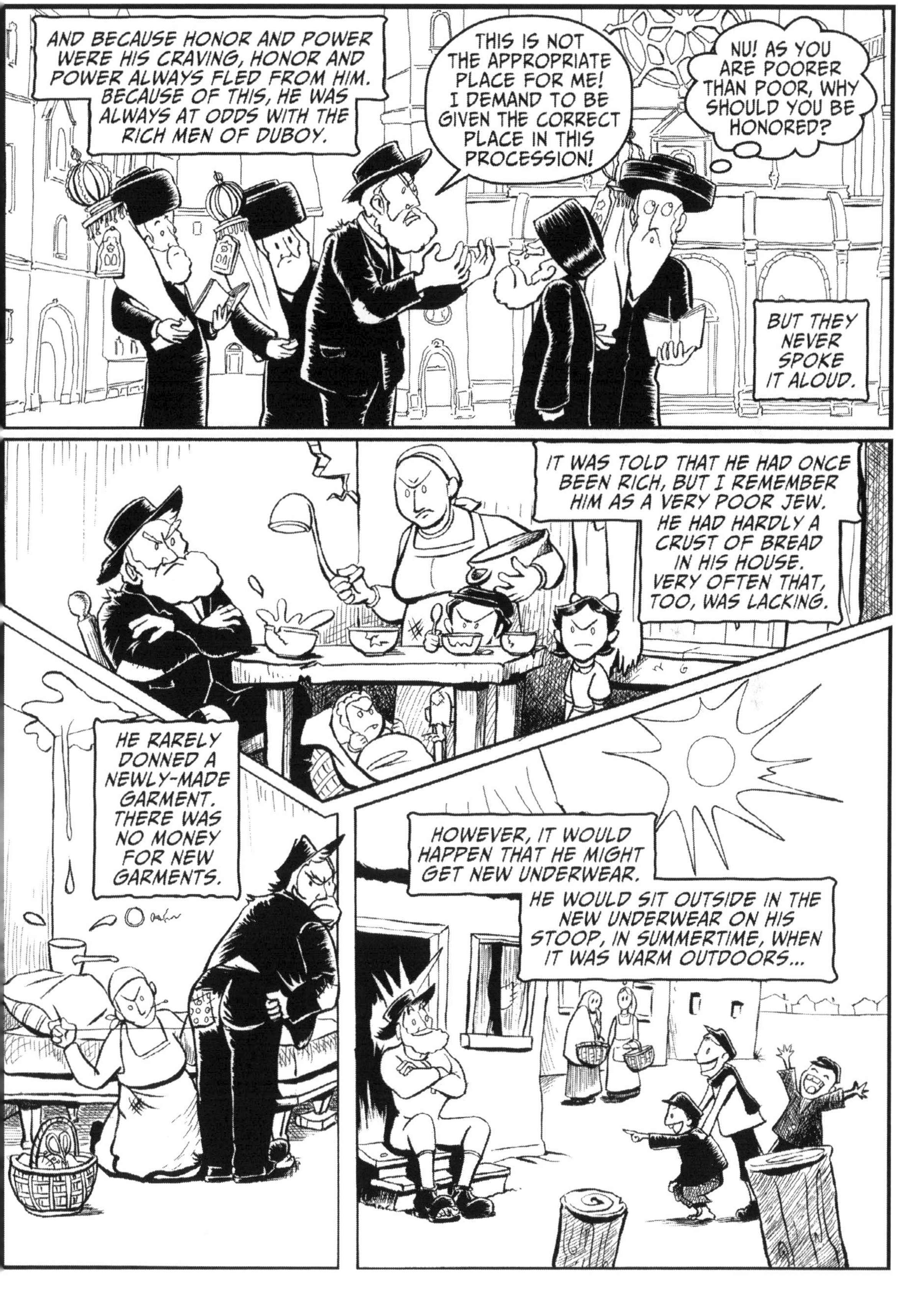
AND BECAUSE HONOR AND POWER WERE HIS CRAVING, HONOR AND POWER ALWAYS FLED FROM HIM.
BECAUSE OF THIS, HE WAS ALWAYS AT ODDS WITH THE RICH MEN OF DUBOY.
THIS IS NOT THE APPROPRIATE PLACE FOR ME! I DEMAND TO BE GIVEN THE CORRECT PLACE IN THIS PROCESSION!
NU! AS YOU ARE POORER THAN POOR, WHY SHOULD YOU BE HONORED?
BUT THEY NEVER SPOKE IT ALOUD.
IT WAS TOLD THAT HE HAD ONCE BEEN RICH, BUT I REMEMBER HIM AS A VERY POOR JEW.
HE HAD HARDLY A CRUST OF BREAD IN HIS HOUSE. VERY OFTEN THAT, TOO, WAS LACKING.
HE RARELY DONNED A NEWLY-MADE GARMENT. THERE WAS NO MONEY FOR NEW GARMENTS.
HOWEVER, IT WOULD HAPPEN THAT HE MIGHT GET NEW UNDERWEAR.
HE WOULD SIT OUTSIDE IN THE NEW UNDERWEAR ON HIS STOOP, IN SUMMERTIME, WHEN IT WAS WARM OUTDOORS...

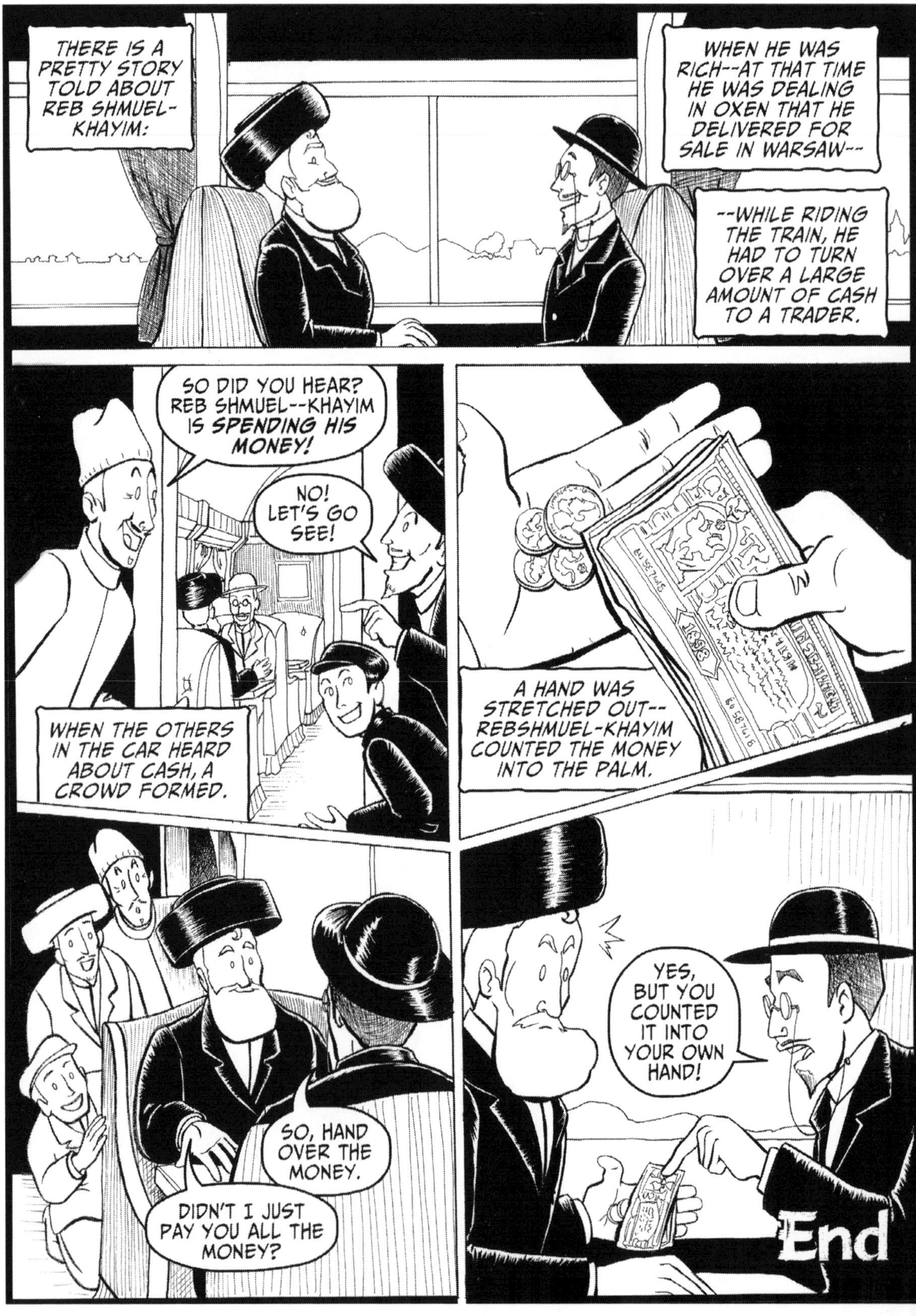
THERE IS A PRETTY STORY TOLD ABOUT REB SHMUEL-KHAYIM:
WHEN HE WAS RICH--AT THAT TIME HE WAS DEALING IN OXEN THAT HE DELIVERED FOR SALE IN WARSAW--
--WHILE RIDING THE TRAIN, HE HAD TO TURN OVER A LARGE AMOUNT OF CASH TO A TRADER.
SO DID YOU HEAR? REB SHMUEL--KHAYIM IS SPENDING HIS MONEY!
NO! LET'S GO SEE!
WHEN THE OTHERS IN THE CAR HEARD ABOUT CASH, A CROWD FORMED.
A HAND WAS STRETCHED OUT-- REBSHMUEL-KHAYIM COUNTED THE MONEY INTO THE PALM.
SO, HAND OVER THE MONEY.
DIDN'T I JUST PAY YOU ALL THE MONEY?
YES, BUT YOU COUNTED IT INTO YOUR OWN HAND!
End

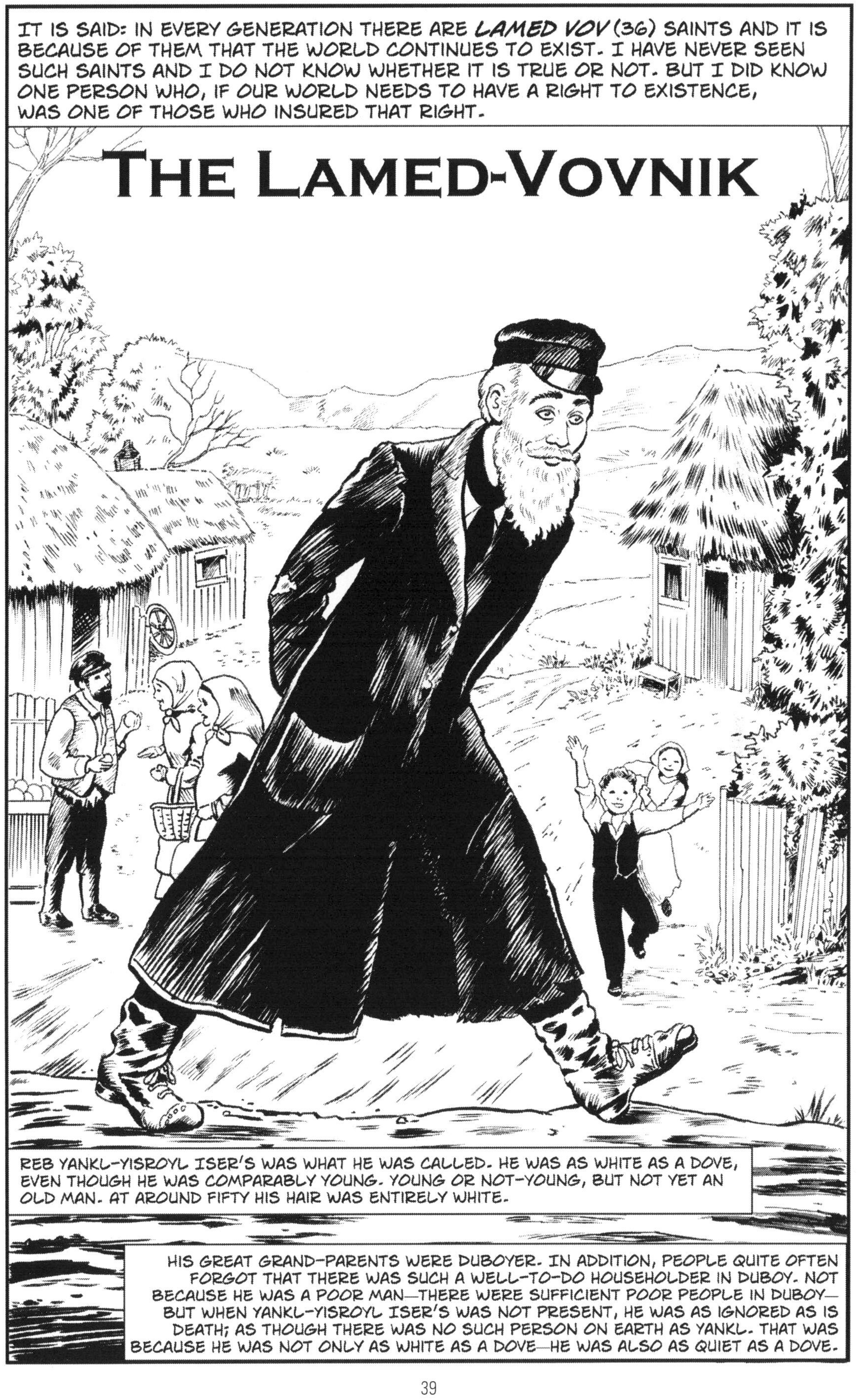
IT IS SAID: IN EVERY GENERATION THERE ARE *LAMED VOV* (36) SAINTS AND IT IS BECAUSE OF THEM THAT THE WORLD CONTINUES TO EXIST. I HAVE NEVER SEEN SUCH SAINTS AND I DO NOT KNOW WHETHER IT IS TRUE OR NOT. BUT I DID KNOW ONE PERSON WHO, IF OUR WORLD NEEDS TO HAVE A RIGHT TO EXISTENCE, WAS ONE OF THOSE WHO INSURED THAT RIGHT.
THE LAMED-VOVNIK
REB YANKL-YISROYL ISER'S WAS WHAT HE WAS CALLED. HE WAS AS WHITE AS A DOVE, EVEN THOUGH HE WAS COMPARABLY YOUNG. YOUNG OR NOT-YOUNG, BUT NOT YET AN OLD MAN. AT AROUND FIFTY HIS HAIR WAS ENTIRELY WHITE.
HIS GREAT GRAND-PARENTS WERE DUBOYER. IN ADDITION, PEOPLE QUITE OFTEN FORGOT THAT THERE WAS SUCH A WELL-TO-DO HOUSEHOLDER IN DUBOY. NOT BECAUSE HE WAS A POOR MAN—THERE WERE SUFFICIENT POOR PEOPLE IN DUBOY—BUT WHEN YANKL-YISROYL ISER'S WAS NOT PRESENT, HE WAS AS IGNORED AS IS DEATH; AS THOUGH THERE WAS NO SUCH PERSON ON EARTH AS YANKL. THAT WAS BECAUSE HE WAS NOT ONLY AS WHITE AS A DOVE—HE WAS ALSO AS QUIET AS A DOVE.

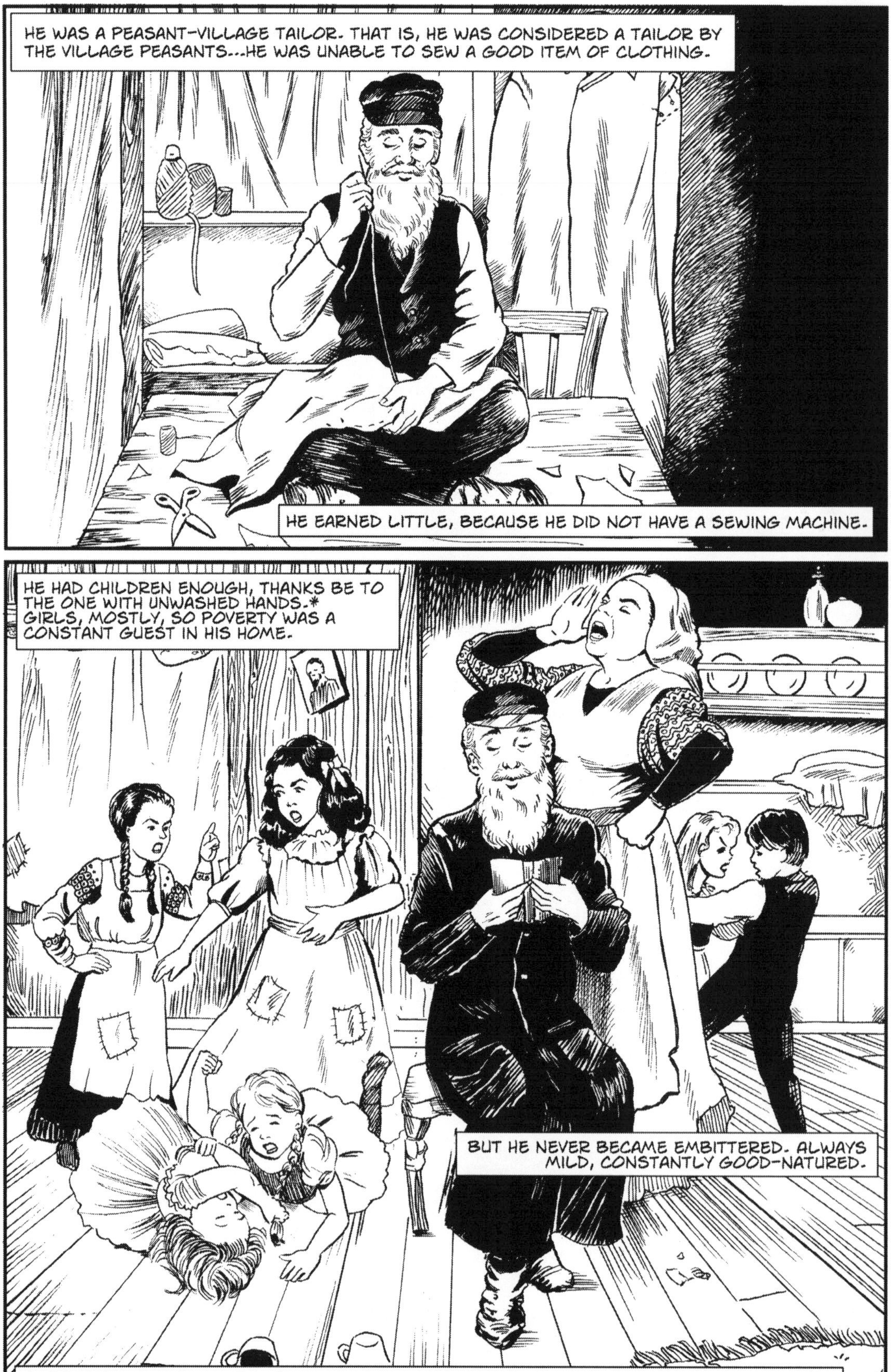
HE WAS A PEASANT-VILLAGE TAILOR. THAT IS, HE WAS CONSIDERED A TAILOR BY THE VILLAGE PEASANTS...HE WAS UNABLE TO SEW A GOOD ITEM OF CLOTHING.
HE EARNED LITTLE, BECAUSE HE DID NOT HAVE A SEWING MACHINE.
HE HAD CHILDREN ENOUGH, THANKS BE TO THE ONE WITH UNWASHED HANDS.* GIRLS, MOSTLY, SO POVERTY WAS A CONSTANT GUEST IN HIS HOME.
BUT HE NEVER BECAME EMBITTERED. ALWAYS MILD, CONSTANTLY GOOD-NATURED.
* SATAN. BUT YOU WOULDN'T WANT TO SAY HIS NAME, BECAUSE HE MIGHT THINK YOU WERE CALLING HIM, AND HE MIGHT COME.

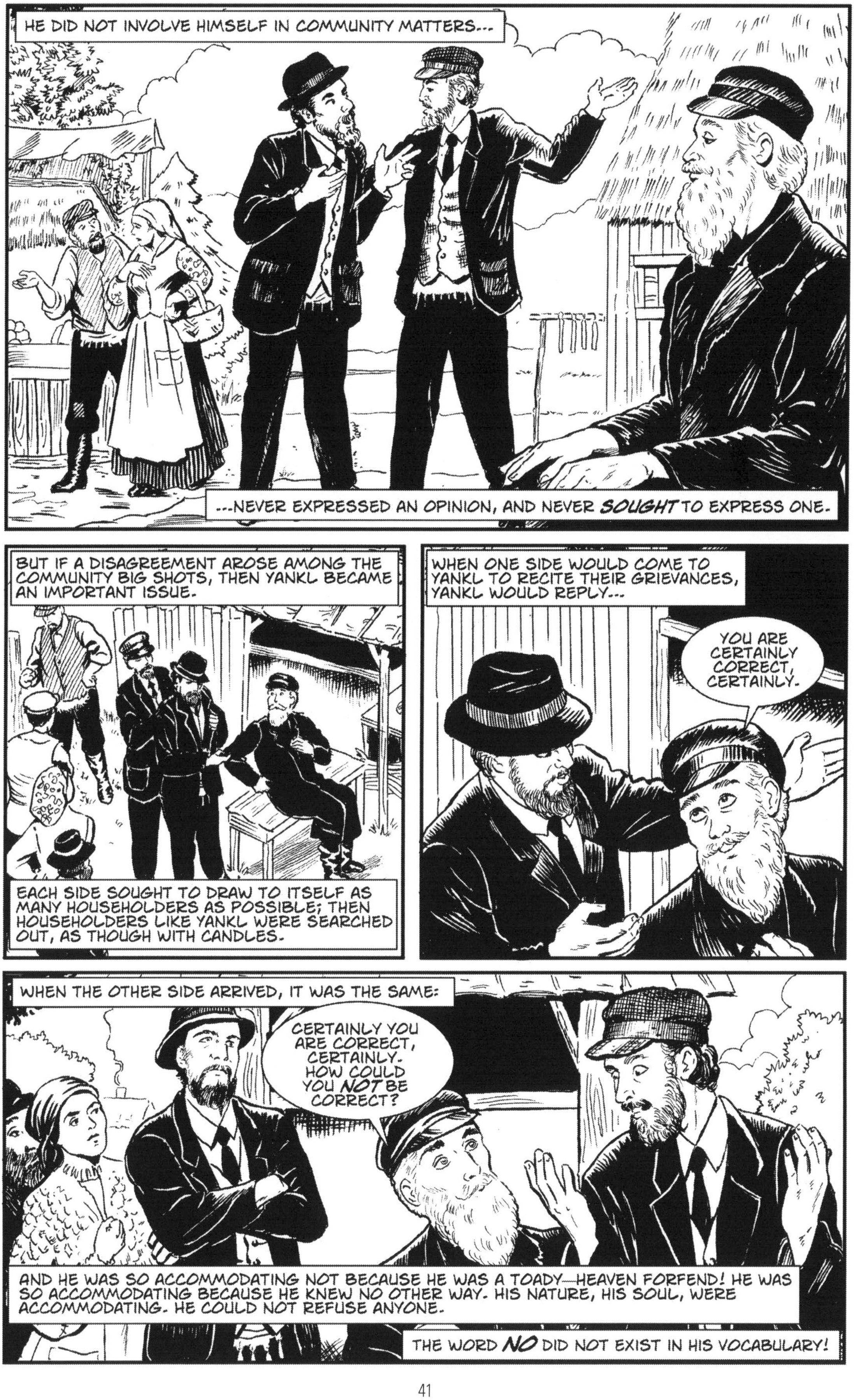
HE DID NOT INVOLVE HIMSELF IN COMMUNITY MATTERS...
...NEVER EXPRESSED AN OPINION, AND NEVER SOUGHT TO EXPRESS ONE.
BUT IF A DISAGREEMENT AROSE AMONG THE COMMUNITY BIG SHOTS, THEN YANKL BECAME AN IMPORTANT ISSUE.
EACH SIDE SOUGHT TO DRAW TO ITSELF AS MANY HOUSEHOLDERS AS POSSIBLE; THEN HOUSEHOLDERS LIKE YANKL WERE SEARCHED OUT, AS THOUGH WITH CANDLES.
WHEN ONE SIDE WOULD COME TO YANKL TO RECITE THEIR GRIEVANCES, YANKL WOULD REPLY...
YOU ARE CERTAINLY CORRECT, CERTAINLY.
WHEN THE OTHER SIDE ARRIVED, IT WAS THE SAME:
CERTAINLY YOU ARE CORRECT, CERTAINLY. HOW COULD YOU NOT BE CORRECT?
AND HE WAS SO ACCOMMODATING NOT BECAUSE HE WAS A TOADY—HEAVEN FORFEND! HE WAS SO ACCOMMODATING BECAUSE HE KNEW NO OTHER WAY. HIS NATURE, HIS SOUL, WERE ACCOMMODATING. HE COULD NOT REFUSE ANYONE.
THE WORD NO DID NOT EXIST IN HIS VOCABULARY!

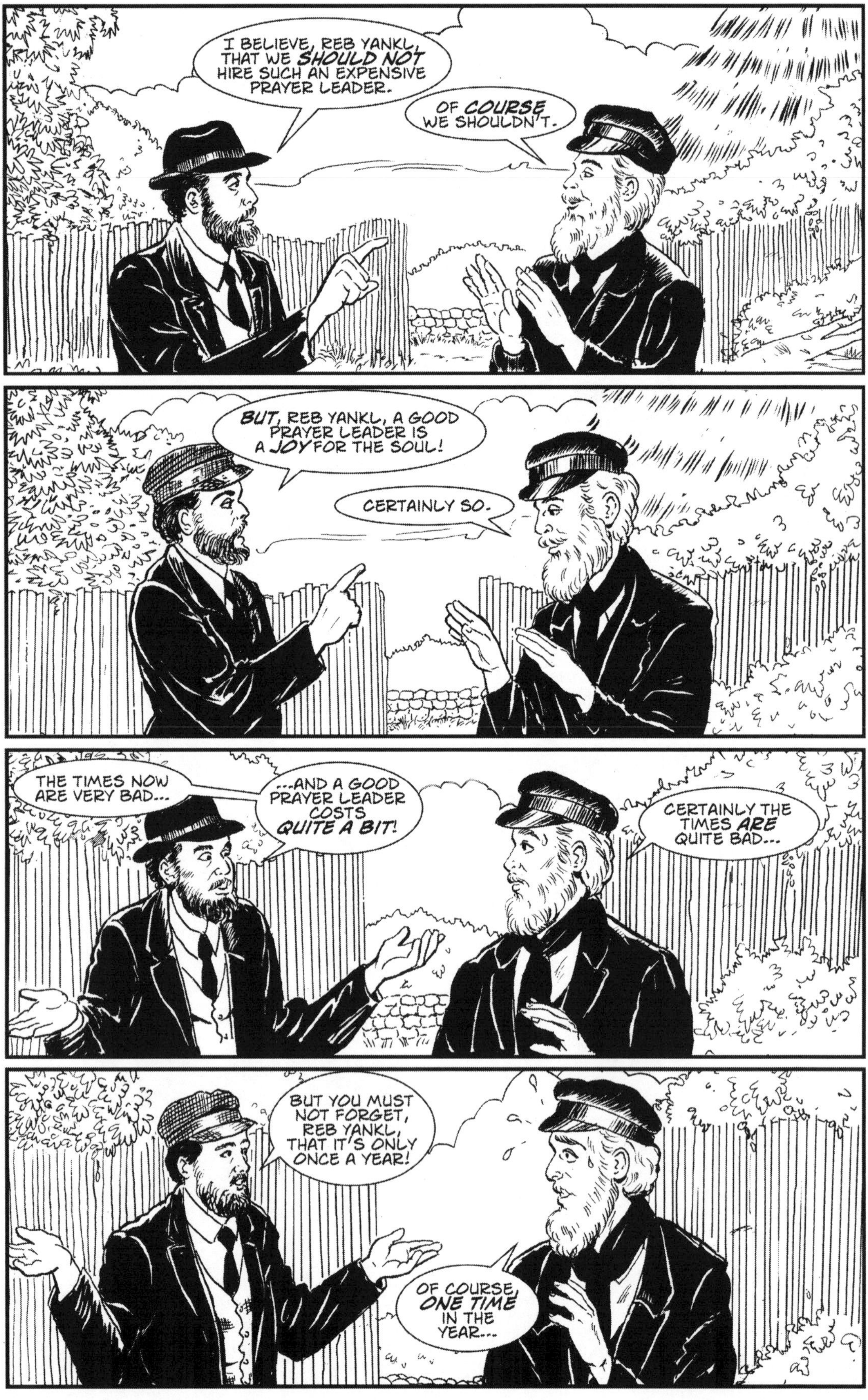
I BELIEVE, REB YANKL, THAT WE SHOULD NOT HIRE SUCH AN EXPENSIVE PRAYER LEADER.
OF COURSE WE SHOULDN'T.
BUT, REB YANKL, A GOOD PRAYER LEADER IS A JOY FOR THE SOUL!
CERTAINLY SO.
THE TIMES NOW ARE VERY BAD...
...AND A GOOD PRAYER LEADER COSTS QUITE A BIT!
CERTAINLY THE TIMES ARE QUITE BAD...
BUT YOU MUST NOT FORGET, REB YANKL, THAT IT'S ONLY ONCE A YEAR!
OF COURSE, ONE TIME IN THE YEAR...

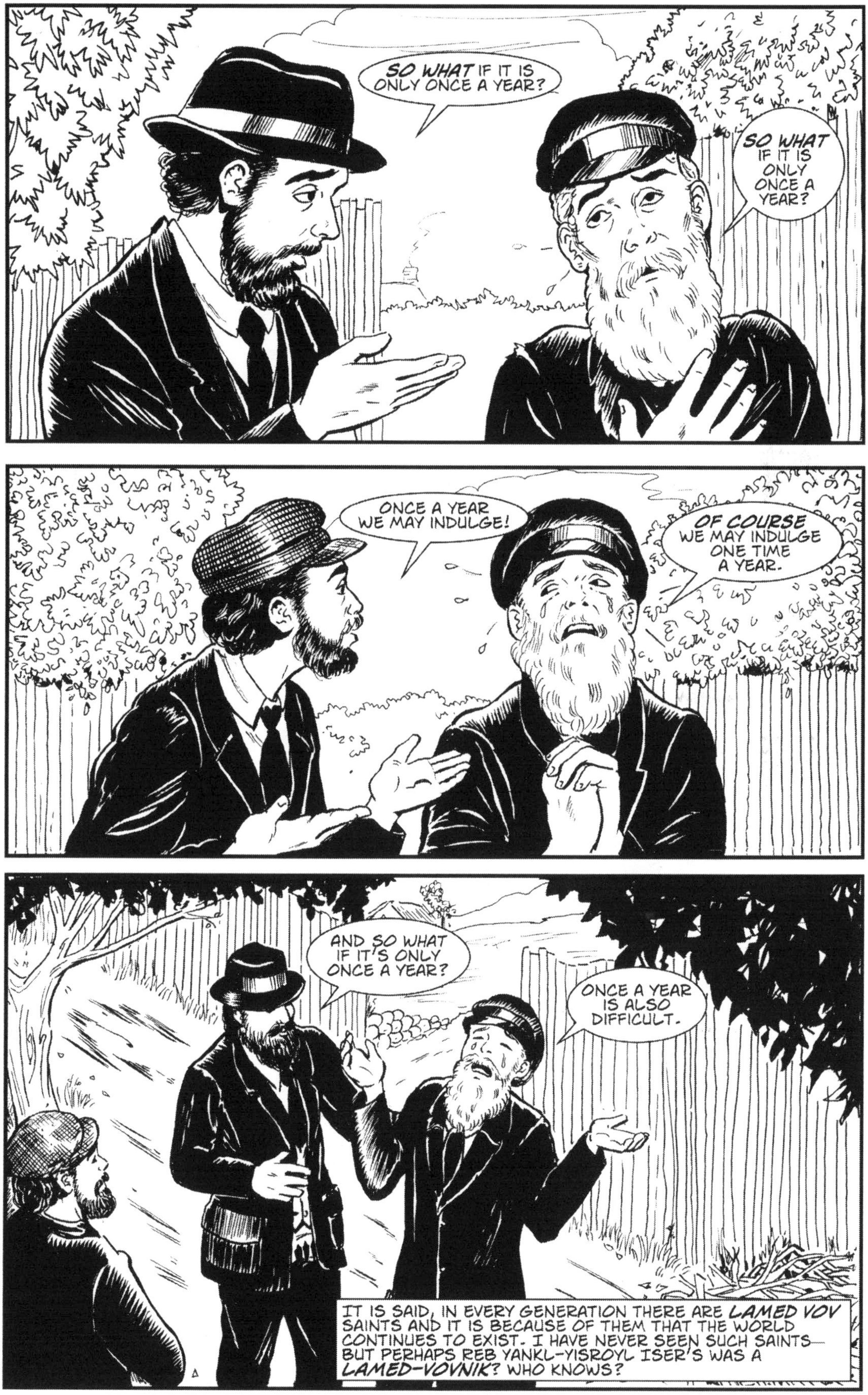
SO WHAT IF IT IS ONLY ONCE A YEAR?
SO WHAT IF IT IS ONLY ONCE A YEAR?
ONCE A YEAR WE MAY INDULGE!
OF COURSE WE MAY INDULGE ONE TIME A YEAR.
AND SO WHAT IF IT'S ONLY ONCE A YEAR?
ONCE A YEAR IS ALSO DIFFICULT.
IT IS SAID, IN EVERY GENERATION THERE ARE LAMED VOV SAINTS AND IT IS BECAUSE OF THEM THAT THE WORLD CONTINUES TO EXIST. I HAVE NEVER SEEN SUCH SAINTS BUT PERHAPS REB YANKL-YISROYL ISER'S WAS A LAMED-VOVNIK? WHO KNOWS?

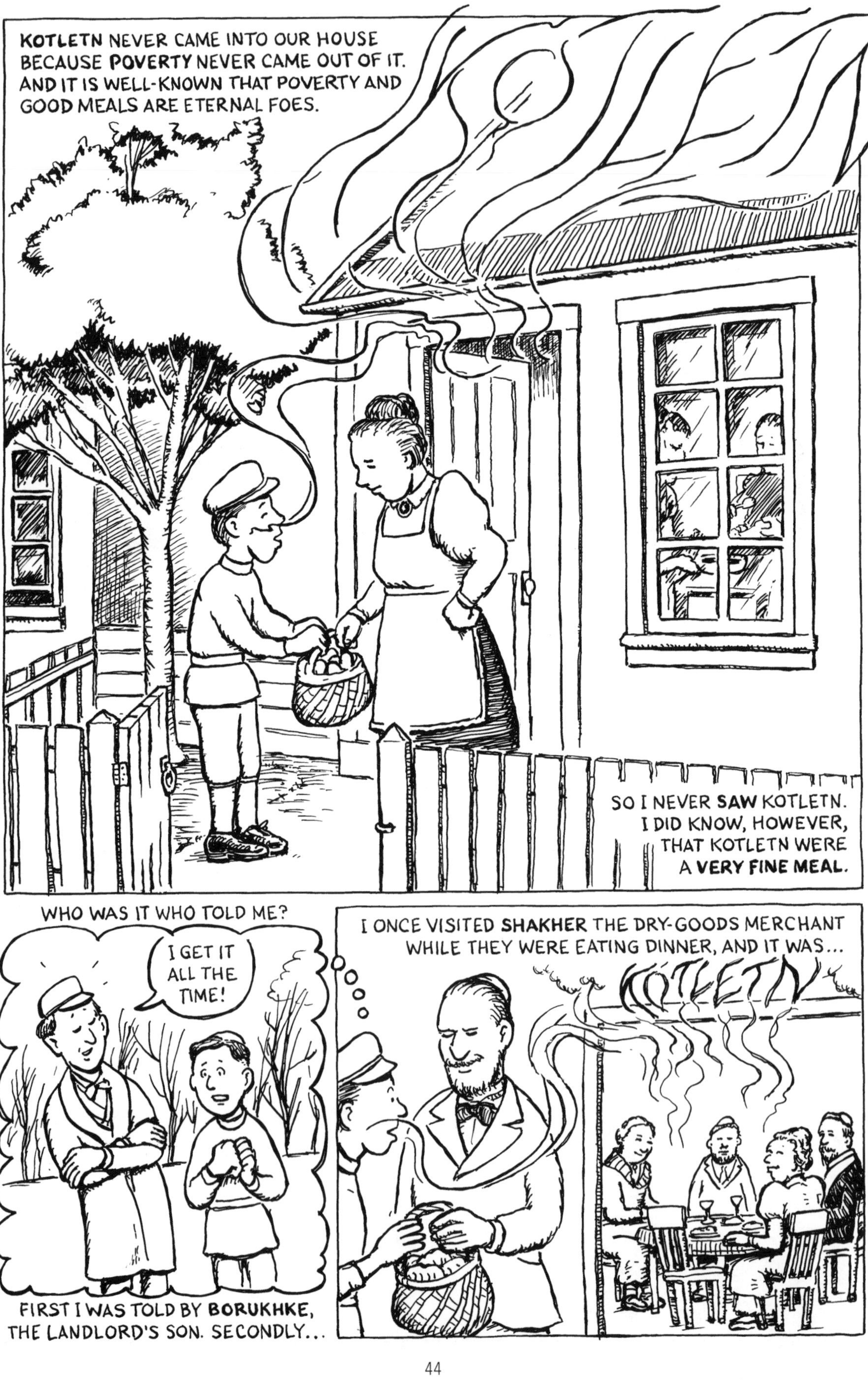
KOTLETN NEVER CAME INTO OUR HOUSE BECAUSE **POVERTY** NEVER CAME OUT OF IT. AND IT IS WELL-KNOWN THAT POVERTY AND GOOD MEALS ARE ETERNAL FOES.
SO I NEVER **SAW** KOTLETN. I DID KNOW, HOWEVER, THAT KOTLETN WERE A **VERY FINE MEAL**.
WHO WAS IT WHO TOLD ME?
I GET IT ALL THE TIME!
FIRST I WAS TOLD BY **BORUKHKE**, THE LANDLORD'S SON. SECONDLY...
I ONCE VISITED **SHAKHER** THE DRY-GOODS MERCHANT WHILE THEY WERE EATING DINNER, AND IT WAS...
KOTLETN

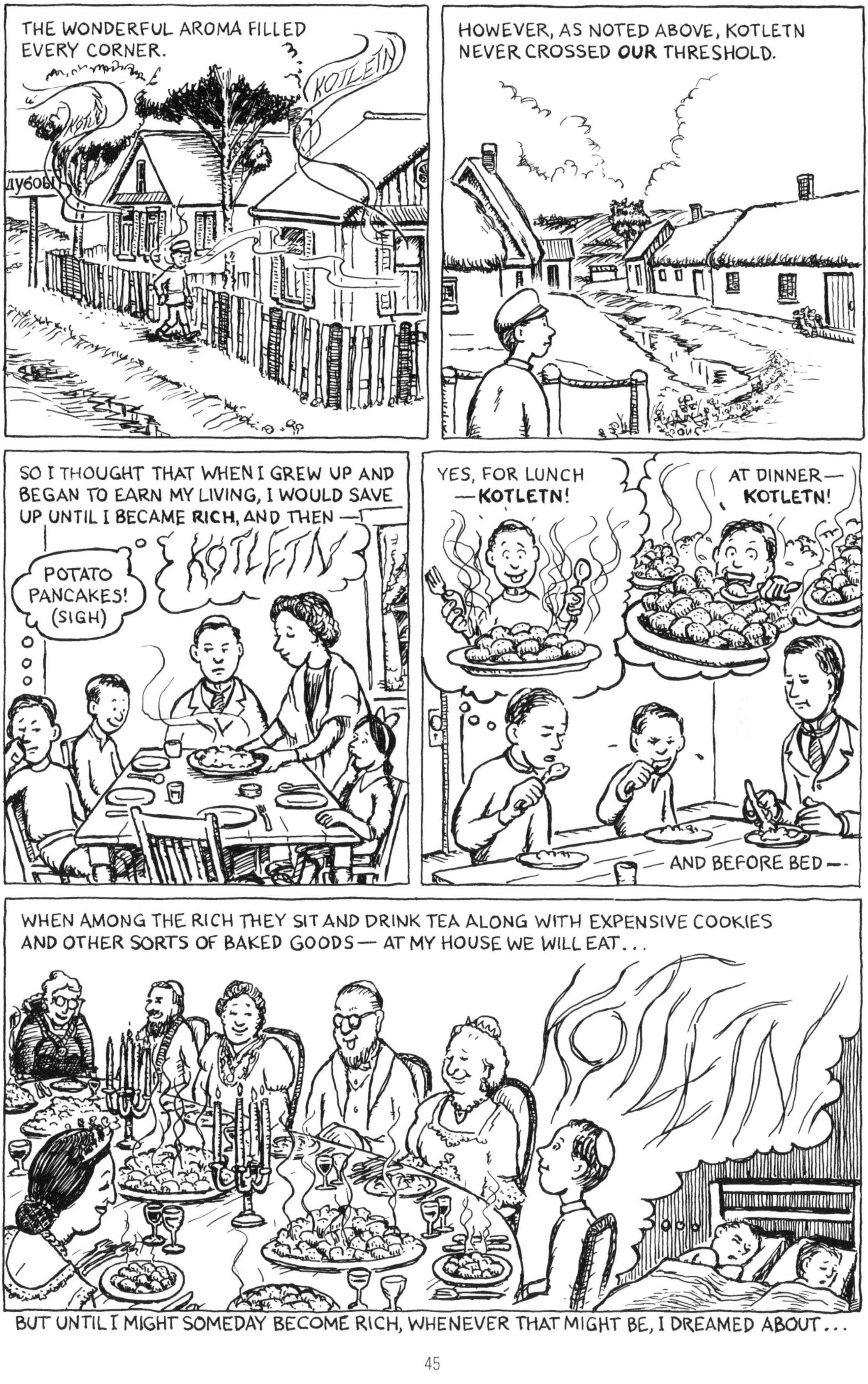
THE WONDERFUL AROMA FILLED EVERY CORNER.
KOTLETN
ДУБОВЫ
HOWEVER, AS NOTED ABOVE, KOTLETN NEVER CROSSED **OUR** THRESHOLD.
SO I THOUGHT THAT WHEN I GREW UP AND BEGAN TO EARN MY LIVING, I WOULD SAVE UP UNTIL I BECAME **RICH**, AND THEN —
KOTLETN
POTATO PANCAKES! (SIGH)
YES, FOR LUNCH —**KOTLETN**!
AT DINNER— **KOTLETN**!
— AND BEFORE BED —.
WHEN AMONG THE RICH THEY SIT AND DRINK TEA ALONG WITH EXPENSIVE COOKIES AND OTHER SORTS OF BAKED GOODS — AT MY HOUSE WE WILL EAT...
KOTLETN
BUT UNTIL I MIGHT SOMEDAY BECOME RICH, WHENEVER THAT MIGHT BE, I DREAMED ABOUT...

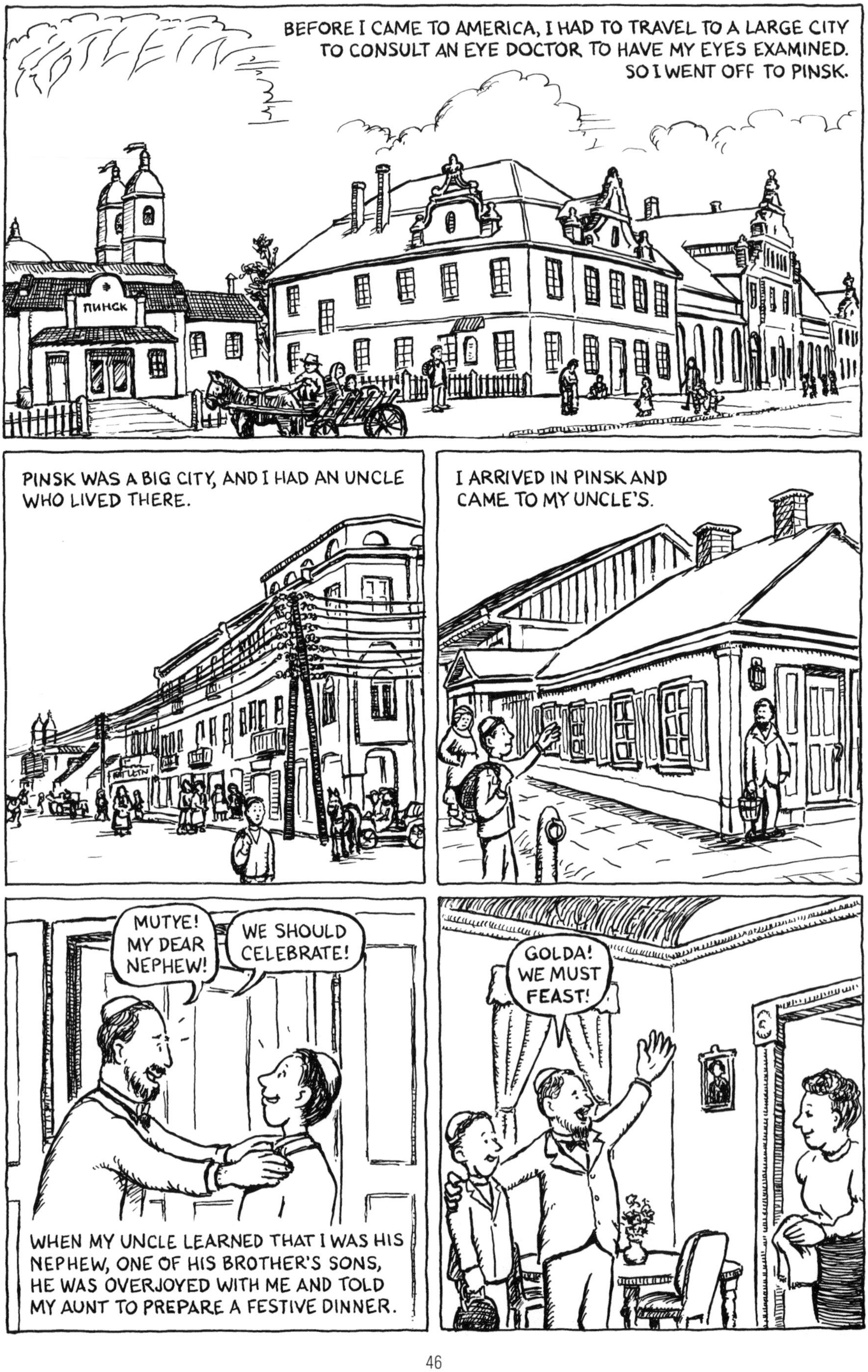
BEFORE I CAME TO AMERICA, I HAD TO TRAVEL TO A LARGE CITY TO CONSULT AN EYE DOCTOR TO HAVE MY EYES EXAMINED. SO I WENT OFF TO PINSK.
ПИНСК
PINSK WAS A BIG CITY, AND I HAD AN UNCLE WHO LIVED THERE.
I ARRIVED IN PINSK AND CAME TO MY UNCLE'S.
MUTYE! MY DEAR NEPHEW!
WE SHOULD CELEBRATE!
WHEN MY UNCLE LEARNED THAT I WAS HIS NEPHEW, ONE OF HIS BROTHER'S SONS, HE WAS OVERJOYED WITH ME AND TOLD MY AUNT TO PREPARE A FESTIVE DINNER.
GOLDA! WE MUST FEAST!

MEANWHILE, I WENT OFF TO AN EYE DOCTOR.
ОКУЛИСТ
глазной врач
котлетн
THE DOCTOR PUT SOME DROPS INTO MY EYES.
К
ОТ
лЕТН
котлетн
—WHICH BROUGHT DARKNESS BEFORE MY EYES!
I BECAME ALARMED!
HOWEVER, THE DOCTOR CALMED ME.
YOU NEED NOT BE ALARMED, IT WILL LAST ONLY A DAY OR TWO, AND THEN YOU WILL BE ABLE TO SEE AS BEFORE...
NEXT!
WHEN I RETURNED FROM THE DOCTOR'S THE TABLE WAS QUICKLY SET. FROM THE KITCHEN, A FAMILIAR AROMA REACHED MY NOSTRILS.
KOTLETN!

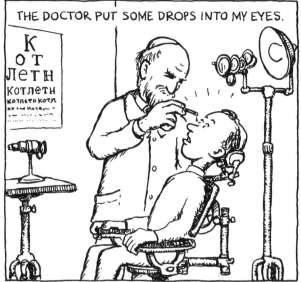

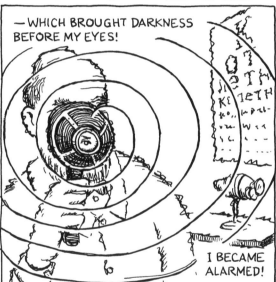

MY AUNT DID NOT KEEP ME WONDERING FOR TOO LONG. SHE ENTERED BEARING TWO PLATES, ONE FOR MY UNCLE AND ONE FOR ME, ON EACH OF WHICH LAY...

KOTLETN

KOTLETN

KOTLETN!

POTATO PANCAKES?! FOR CRYING OUT LOUD!

TO YOUR OWN BROTHER'S CHILD WHOM YOU HAVE NEVER BEFORE SEEN, AND GOD KNOWS WHETHER YOU WILL EVER SEE AGAIN, YOU PRESENT **POTATO PANCAKES!**

THEY COULDN'T MAKE A ROAST IN MY HONOR, OR EVEN ACTUAL **KOTLETN?**

WOULD THEY REALLY BECOME **POOR,** GOD FORBID?

I'M — I'M NOT HUNGRY.

AFTER DINNER, IN MY BEDROOM, I HEARD MY AUNT SPEAKING WITH MY UNCLE:

WHAT **GRAND FOOD** MUST THEY EAT BACK AT HIS HOME...!

RUMBLE RUMBLE

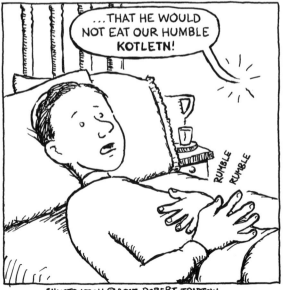

...THAT HE WOULD NOT EAT OUR HUMBLE **KOTLETN!**

RUMBLE RUMBLE

ILLUSTRATION © 2017 ROBERT TRIPTOW

JUST AS EGGS ARE AS GOOD AS MEAT ~ SO TASTY, EVEN WITHOUT SHMALTS ~ SO TASTY, THAT ONE MIGHT CONCLUDE: HOW GOOD IT MUST BE WHEN MEAT IS GROUND UP & EGGS ARE BEATEN INTO IT, & IT'S EVEN FRIED IN SHMALTS!

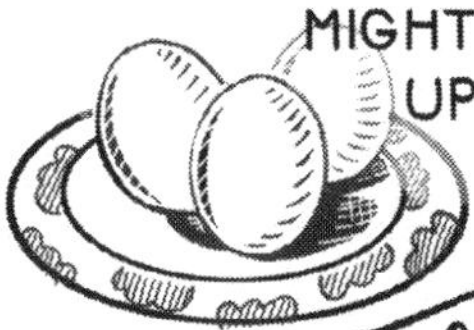

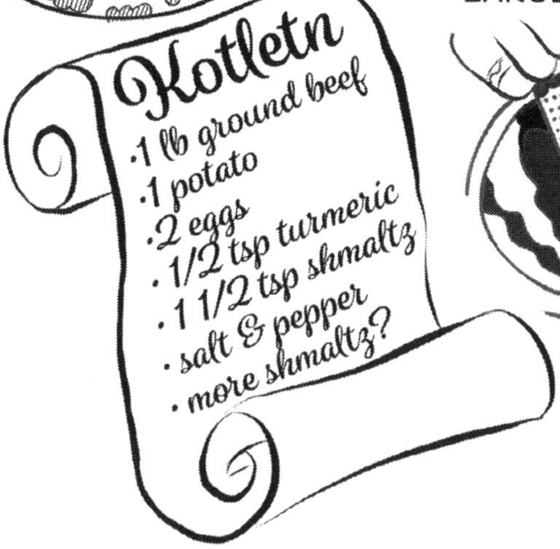
Kotletn
·1 lb ground beef
·1 potato
·2 eggs
·1/2 tsp turmeric
·1 1/2 tsp shmaltz
·salt & pepper
·more shmaltz?

GRATE ONION & POTATO IN A LARGE BOWL. MIX TO COMBINE.

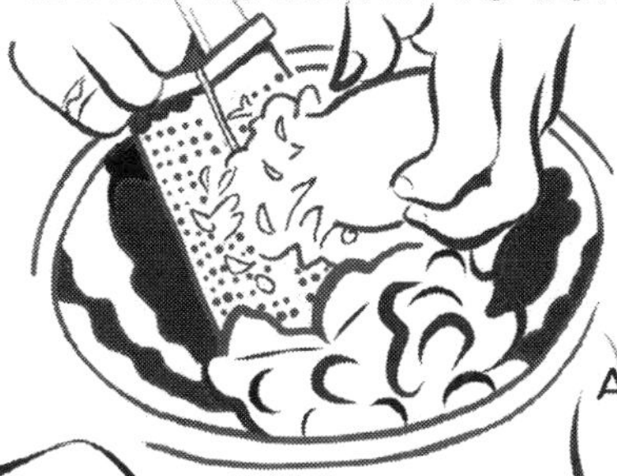

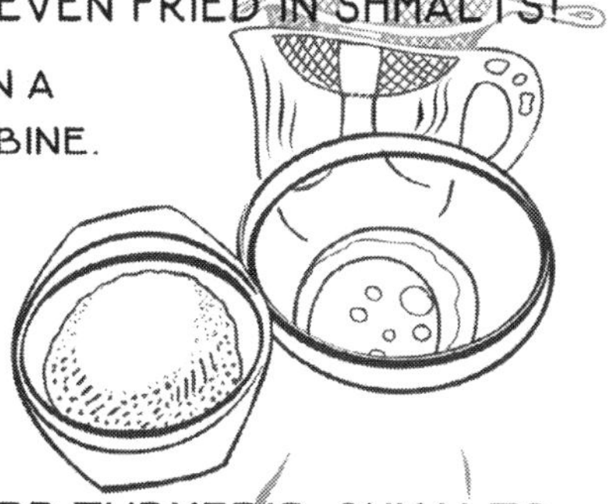

ADD TURMERIC, SHMALTS, SALT & PEPPER.

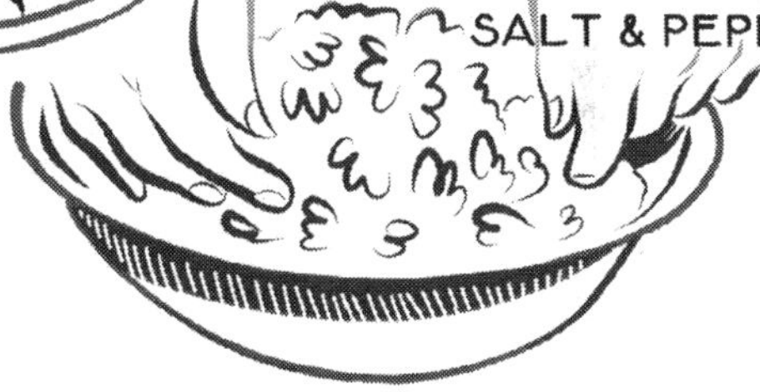

MIX TO INCORPORATE SPICES INTO POTATO~ONION MIXTURE.

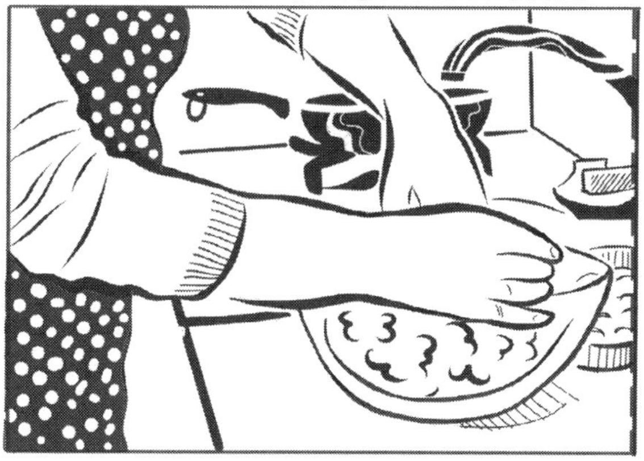

CRACK EGGS INTO THE MIXTURE, AND COMBINE.

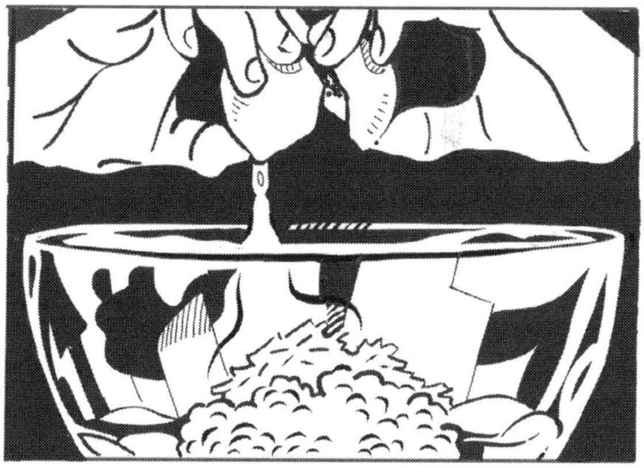

FINALLY, ADD THE GROUND BEEF TO THE MIXTURE ~ AND MIX!

(AGAIN, KEEP MIXING AT IT WITH THE HANDS!)

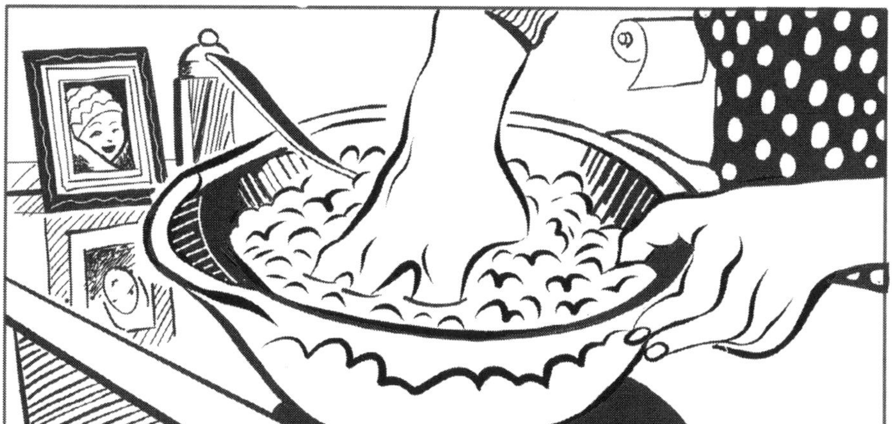

TAKE A SMALL AMOUNT OF THE MIXTURE (ABOUT 2 TBSP) & MAKE A LARGE MEATBALL WITH IT. PAT IT FLAT INTO A PATTY THAT'S NOT TOO THICK OR TOO THIN.

WASH YOUR HANDS, AND HEAT SHMALTS IN A LARGE PAN OVER MEDIUM HEAT. FRY A FEW KOTLETN AT A TIME, MAKING SURE NOT TO OVERCROWD.

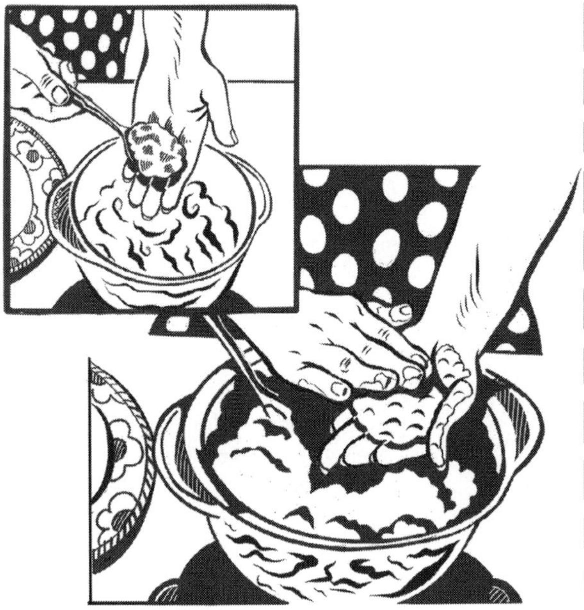

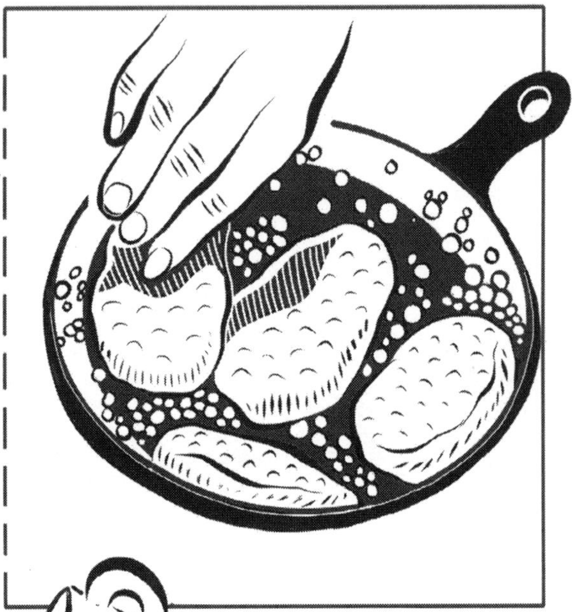

ONCE YOU SEE THE BOTTOM HAS TURNED A GOLDEN BROWN WHERE THE EDGES ARE BROWN AND CRISPY, FLIP THEM OVER.

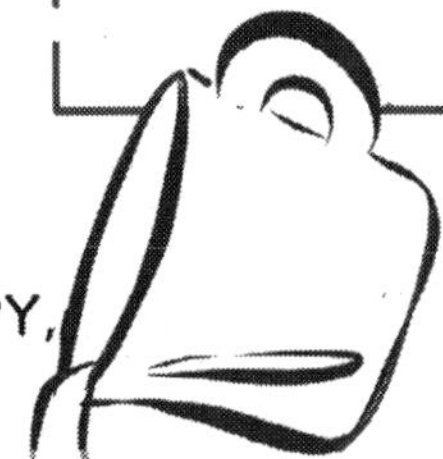
shmaltz

ADD MORE SHMALTS AS NECESSARY.

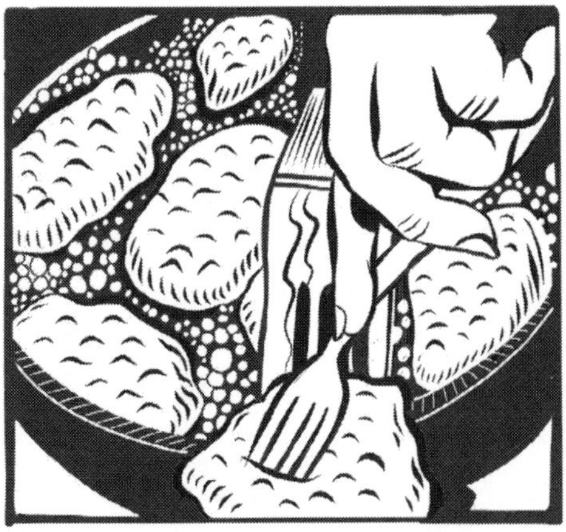

PLACE A DISH WITH A PAPER TOWEL IN IT NEXT TO YOUR WORK STATION.

WHEN REMOVING KOTLETN FROM THE PAN, TRY TO DRAIN AS MUCH OF THE SHMALTS AS POSSIBLE BEFORE PLACING ONTO THE PLATE.

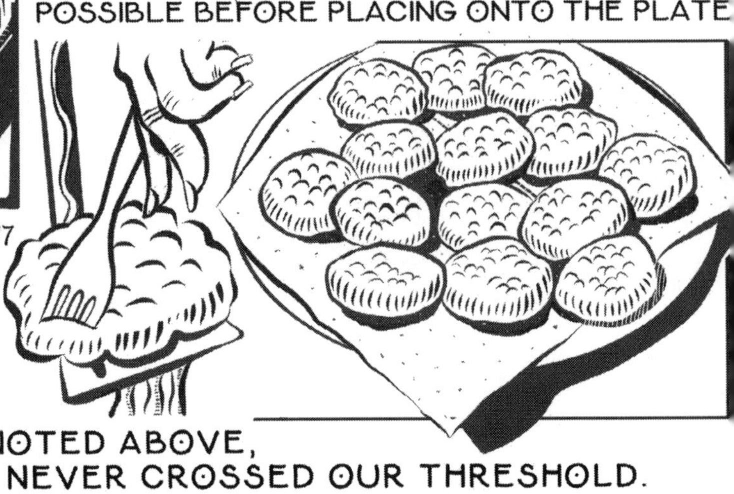

HOWEVER, AS NOTED ABOVE, KOTLETN NEVER CROSSED OUR THRESHOLD.

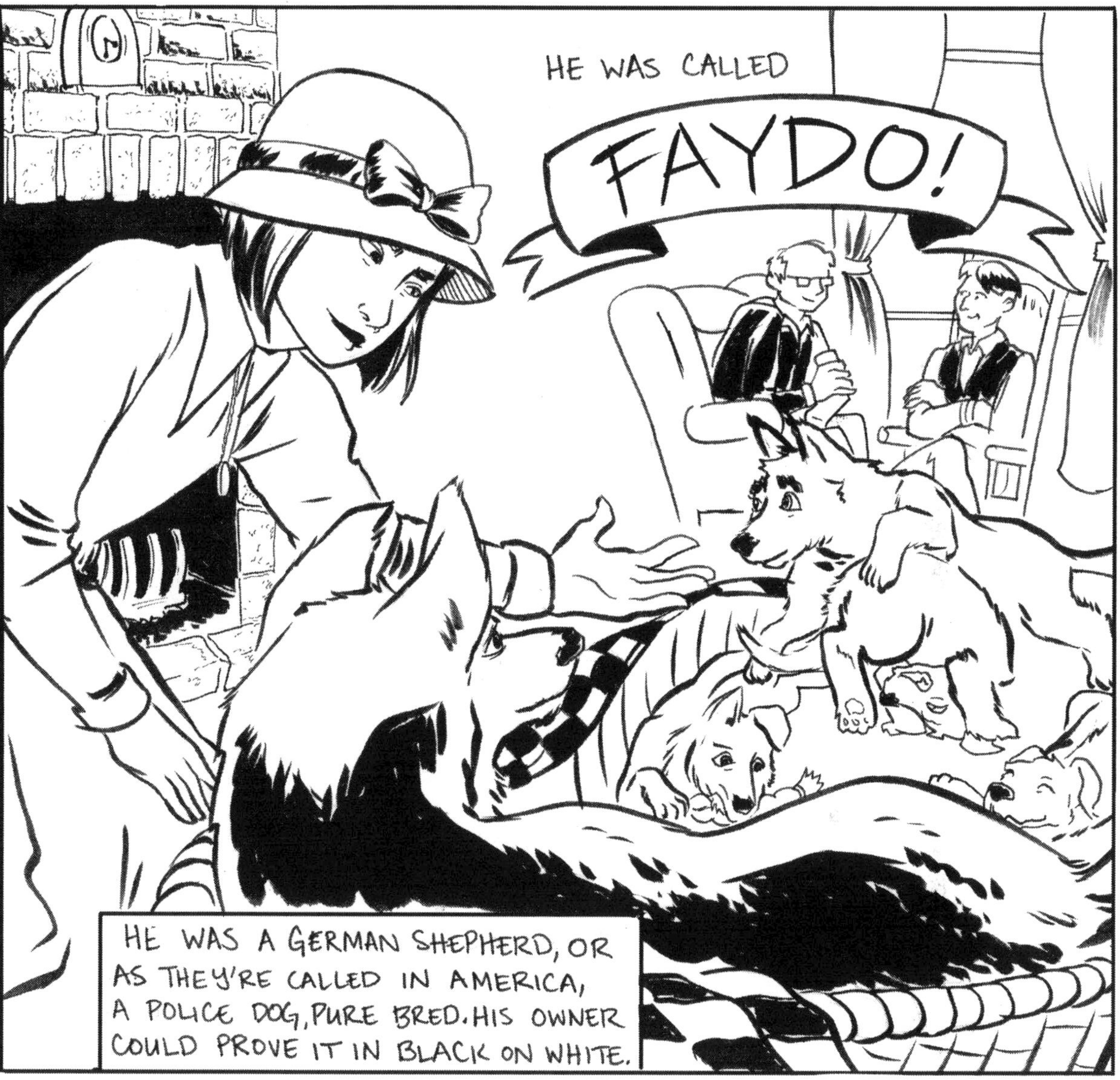
HE WAS CALLED
FAYDO!
HE WAS A GERMAN SHEPHERD, OR AS THEY'RE CALLED IN AMERICA, A POLICE DOG, PURE BRED. HIS OWNER COULD PROVE IT IN BLACK ON WHITE.

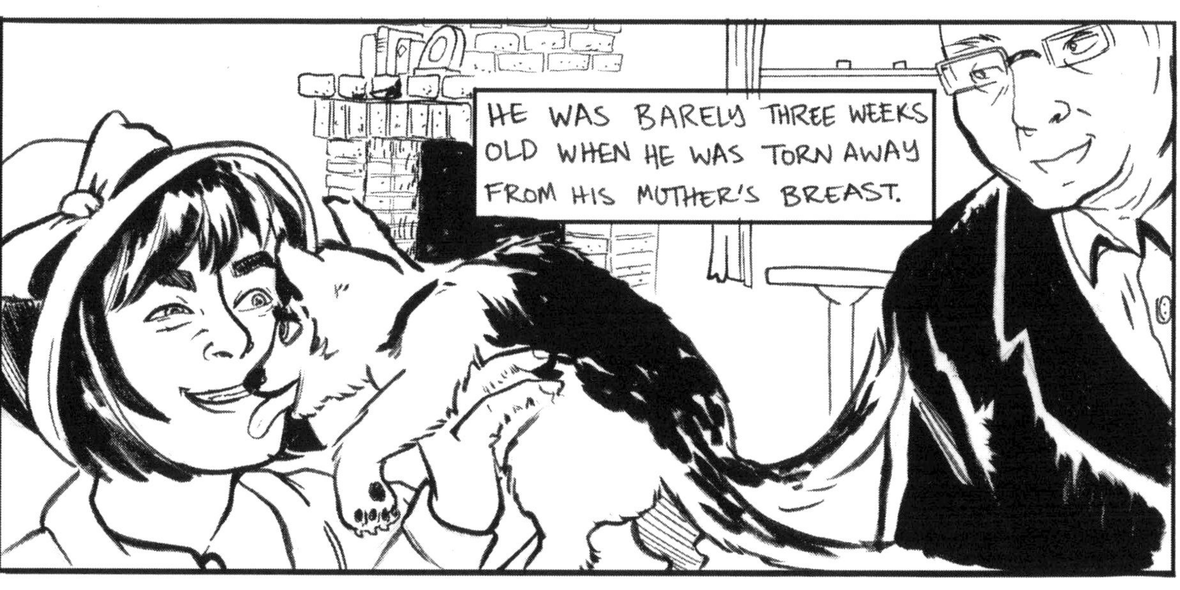
HE WAS BARELY THREE WEEKS OLD WHEN HE WAS TORN AWAY FROM HIS MOTHER'S BREAST.

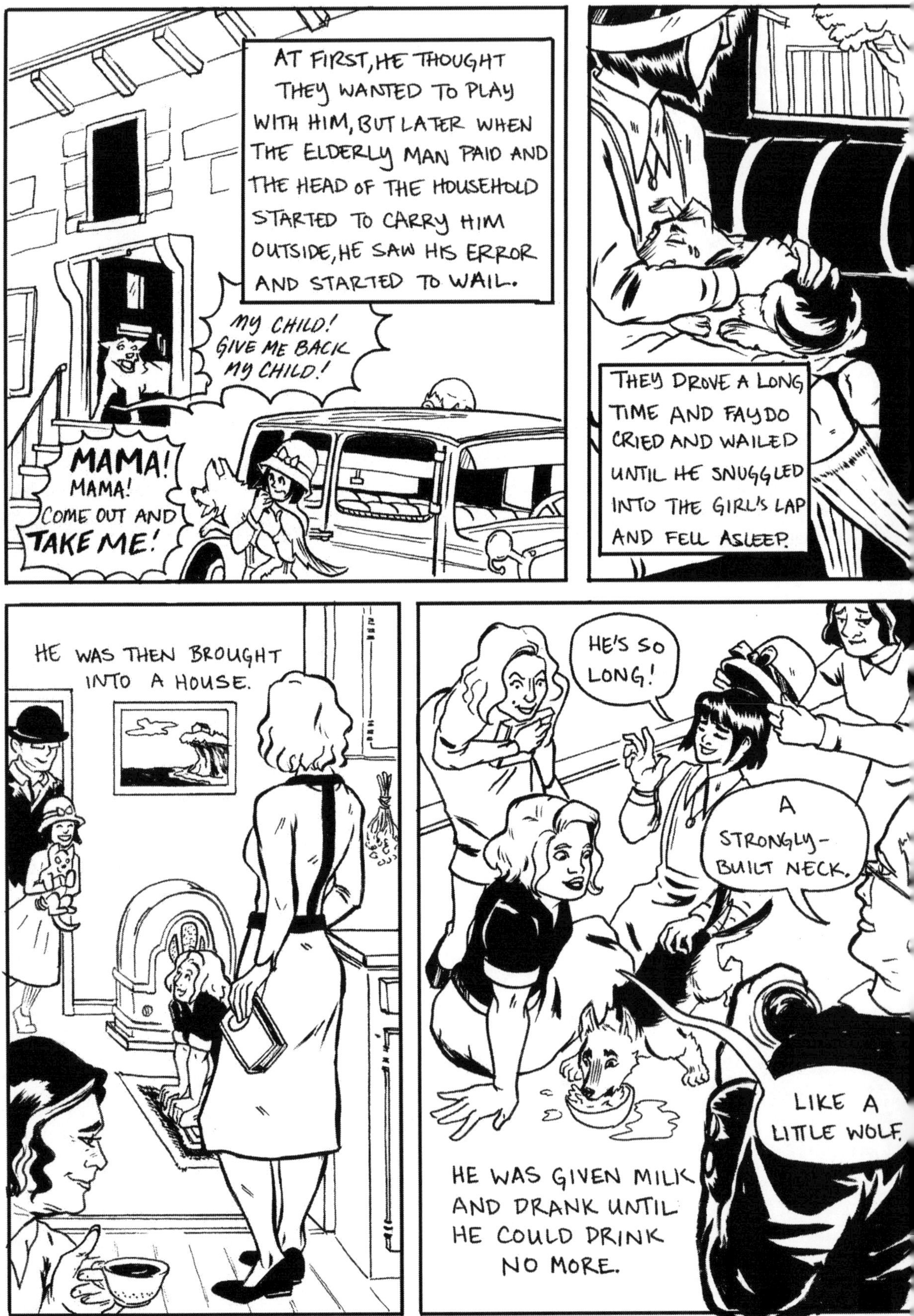
AT FIRST, HE THOUGHT THEY WANTED TO PLAY WITH HIM, BUT LATER WHEN THE ELDERLY MAN PAID AND THE HEAD OF THE HOUSEHOLD STARTED TO CARRY HIM OUTSIDE, HE SAW HIS ERROR AND STARTED TO WAIL.
MY CHILD! GIVE ME BACK MY CHILD!
MAMA! MAMA! COME OUT AND TAKE ME!
THEY DROVE A LONG TIME AND FAYDO CRIED AND WAILED UNTIL HE SNUGGLED INTO THE GIRL'S LAP AND FELL ASLEEP.
HE WAS THEN BROUGHT INTO A HOUSE.
HE'S SO LONG!
A STRONGLY-BUILT NECK.
LIKE A LITTLE WOLF.
HE WAS GIVEN MILK AND DRANK UNTIL HE COULD DRINK NO MORE.

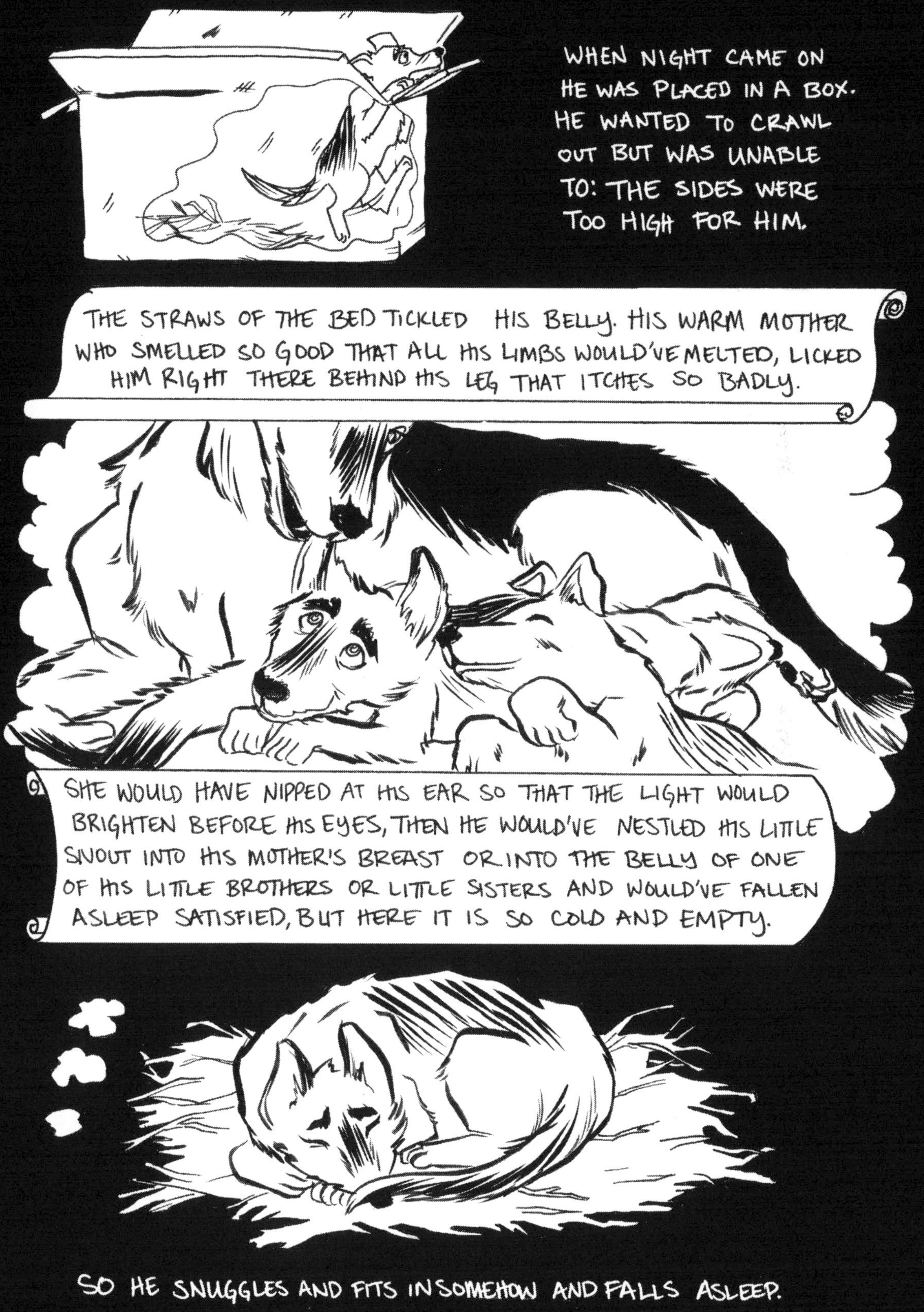
WHEN NIGHT CAME ON HE WAS PLACED IN A BOX. HE WANTED TO CRAWL OUT BUT WAS UNABLE TO: THE SIDES WERE TOO HIGH FOR HIM.
THE STRAWS OF THE BED TICKLED HIS BELLY. HIS WARM MOTHER WHO SMELLED SO GOOD THAT ALL HIS LIMBS WOULD'VE MELTED, LICKED HIM RIGHT THERE BEHIND HIS LEG THAT ITCHES SO BADLY.
SHE WOULD HAVE NIPPED AT HIS EAR SO THAT THE LIGHT WOULD BRIGHTEN BEFORE HIS EYES, THEN HE WOULD'VE NESTLED HIS LITTLE SNOUT INTO HIS MOTHER'S BREAST OR INTO THE BELLY OF ONE OF HIS LITTLE BROTHERS OR LITTLE SISTERS AND WOULD'VE FALLEN ASLEEP SATISFIED, BUT HERE IT IS SO COLD AND EMPTY.
SO HE SNUGGLES AND FITS IN SOMEHOW AND FALLS ASLEEP.

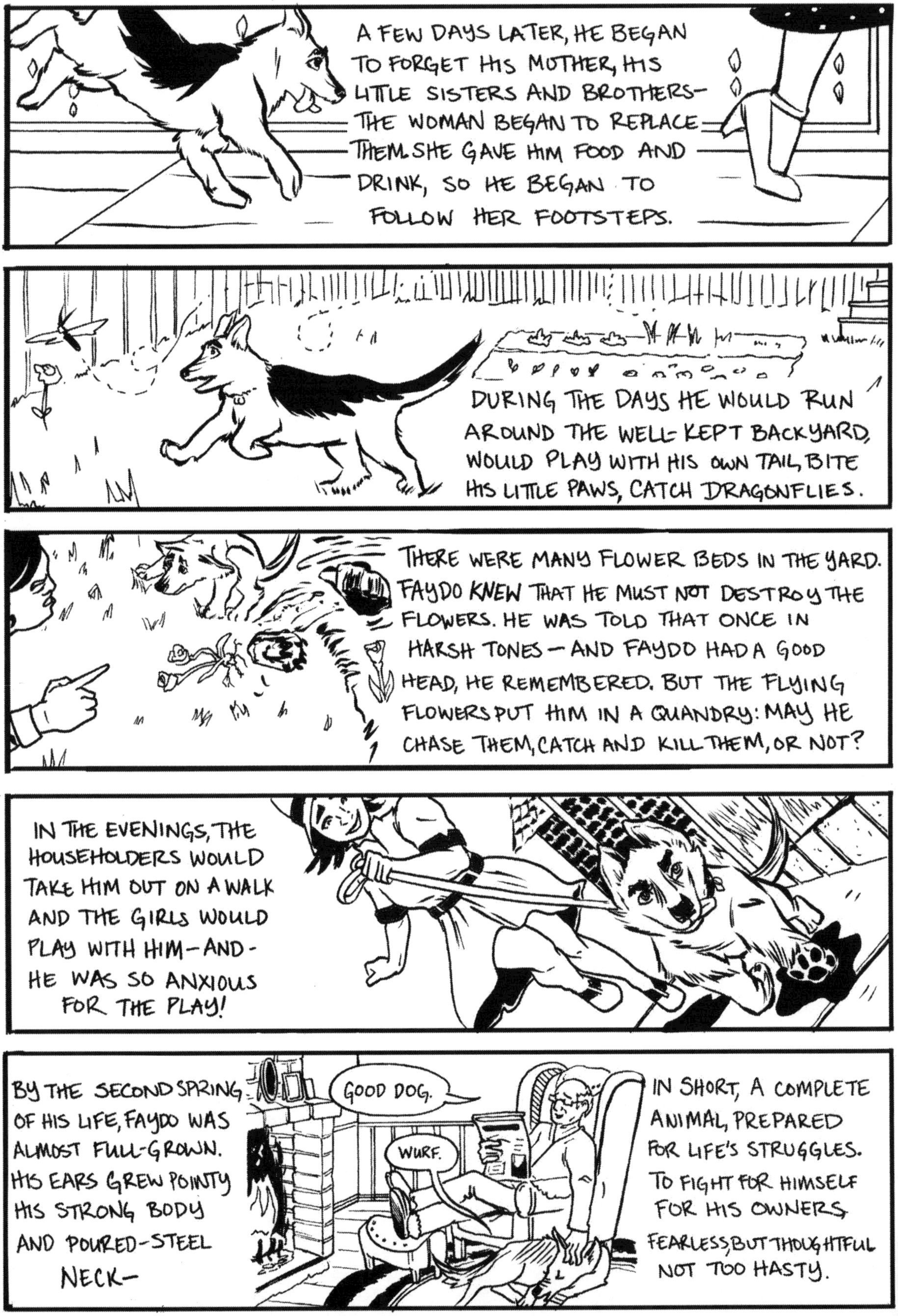
A FEW DAYS LATER, HE BEGAN TO FORGET HIS MOTHER, HIS LITTLE SISTERS AND BROTHERS— THE WOMAN BEGAN TO REPLACE THEM. SHE GAVE HIM FOOD AND DRINK, SO HE BEGAN TO FOLLOW HER FOOTSTEPS.
DURING THE DAYS HE WOULD RUN AROUND THE WELL-KEPT BACKYARD, WOULD PLAY WITH HIS OWN TAIL, BITE HIS LITTLE PAWS, CATCH DRAGONFLIES.
THERE WERE MANY FLOWER BEDS IN THE YARD. FAYDO KNEW THAT HE MUST NOT DESTROY THE FLOWERS. HE WAS TOLD THAT ONCE IN HARSH TONES — AND FAYDO HAD A GOOD HEAD, HE REMEMBERED. BUT THE FLYING FLOWERS PUT HIM IN A QUANDRY: MAY HE CHASE THEM, CATCH AND KILL THEM, OR NOT?
IN THE EVENINGS, THE HOUSEHOLDERS WOULD TAKE HIM OUT ON A WALK AND THE GIRLS WOULD PLAY WITH HIM—AND—HE WAS SO ANXIOUS FOR THE PLAY!
BY THE SECOND SPRING OF HIS LIFE, FAYDO WAS ALMOST FULL-GROWN. HIS EARS GREW POINTY HIS STRONG BODY AND POURED-STEEL NECK—
GOOD DOG.
WURF.
IN SHORT, A COMPLETE ANIMAL, PREPARED FOR LIFE'S STRUGGLES. TO FIGHT FOR HIMSELF FOR HIS OWNERS. FEARLESS, BUT THOUGHTFUL NOT TOO HASTY.

HE IS NOW 11 YEARS OLD. A LONG AGE FOR A DOG. HE EATS, GUARDS THE HOUSEHOLD AND IS TREMENDOUSLY BOUND TO ITS OCCUPANTS SHOULD ONE OF THEM NOT RETURN HOME ONE DAY, HE LIFE WOULD END IN YEARNING.

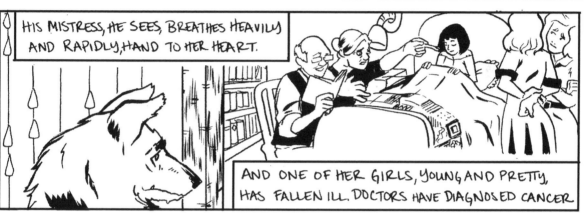

HIS MISTRESS, HE SEES, BREATHES HEAVILY AND RAPIDLY, HAND TO HER HEART.

AND ONE OF HER GIRLS, YOUNG AND PRETTY, HAS FALLEN ILL. DOCTORS HAVE DIAGNOSED CANCER.

ONCE, JUST BEFORE CHRISTMAS, THE AGED HOUSEHOLDER'S WIFE DROVE TO BUY GIFTS FOR THE FAMILY.

THE STORE WAS CROWDED, JAMMED FULL. IT WAS TOO MUCH FOR HER WEAK HEART.

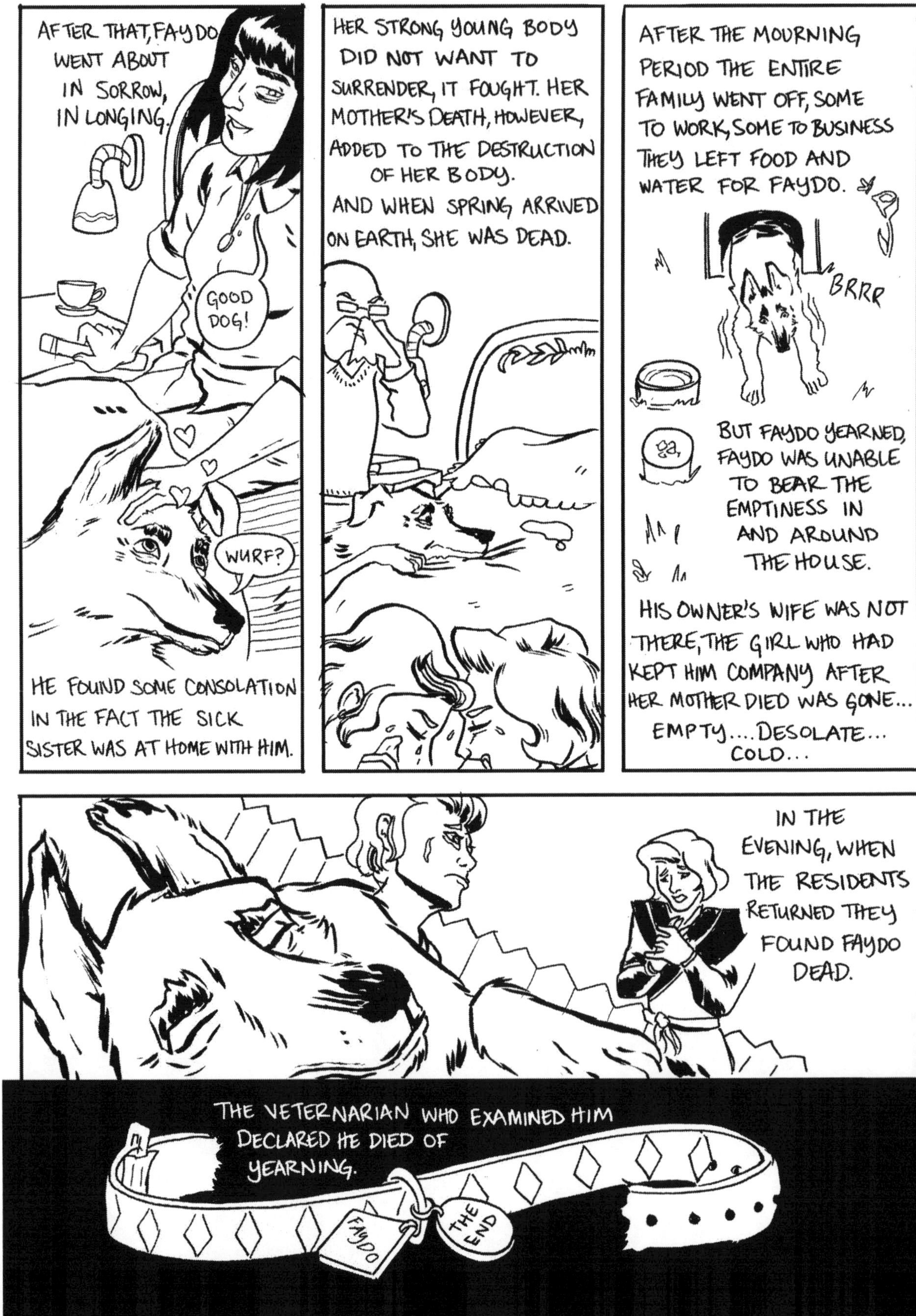
AFTER THAT, FAYDO WENT ABOUT IN SORROW, IN LONGING.
GOOD DOG!
WURF?
HE FOUND SOME CONSOLATION IN THE FACT THE SICK SISTER WAS AT HOME WITH HIM.
HER STRONG YOUNG BODY DID NOT WANT TO SURRENDER, IT FOUGHT. HER MOTHER'S DEATH, HOWEVER, ADDED TO THE DESTRUCTION OF HER BODY.
AND WHEN SPRING ARRIVED ON EARTH, SHE WAS DEAD.
AFTER THE MOURNING PERIOD THE ENTIRE FAMILY WENT OFF, SOME TO WORK, SOME TO BUSINESS THEY LEFT FOOD AND WATER FOR FAYDO.
BRRR
BUT FAYDO YEARNED, FAYDO WAS UNABLE TO BEAR THE EMPTINESS IN AND AROUND THE HOUSE.
HIS OWNER'S WIFE WAS NOT THERE, THE GIRL WHO HAD KEPT HIM COMPANY AFTER HER MOTHER DIED WAS GONE... EMPTY.... DESOLATE... COLD...
IN THE EVENING, WHEN THE RESIDENTS RETURNED THEY FOUND FAYDO DEAD.
THE VETERNARIAN WHO EXAMINED HIM DECLARED HE DIED OF YEARNING.
FAYDO
THE END

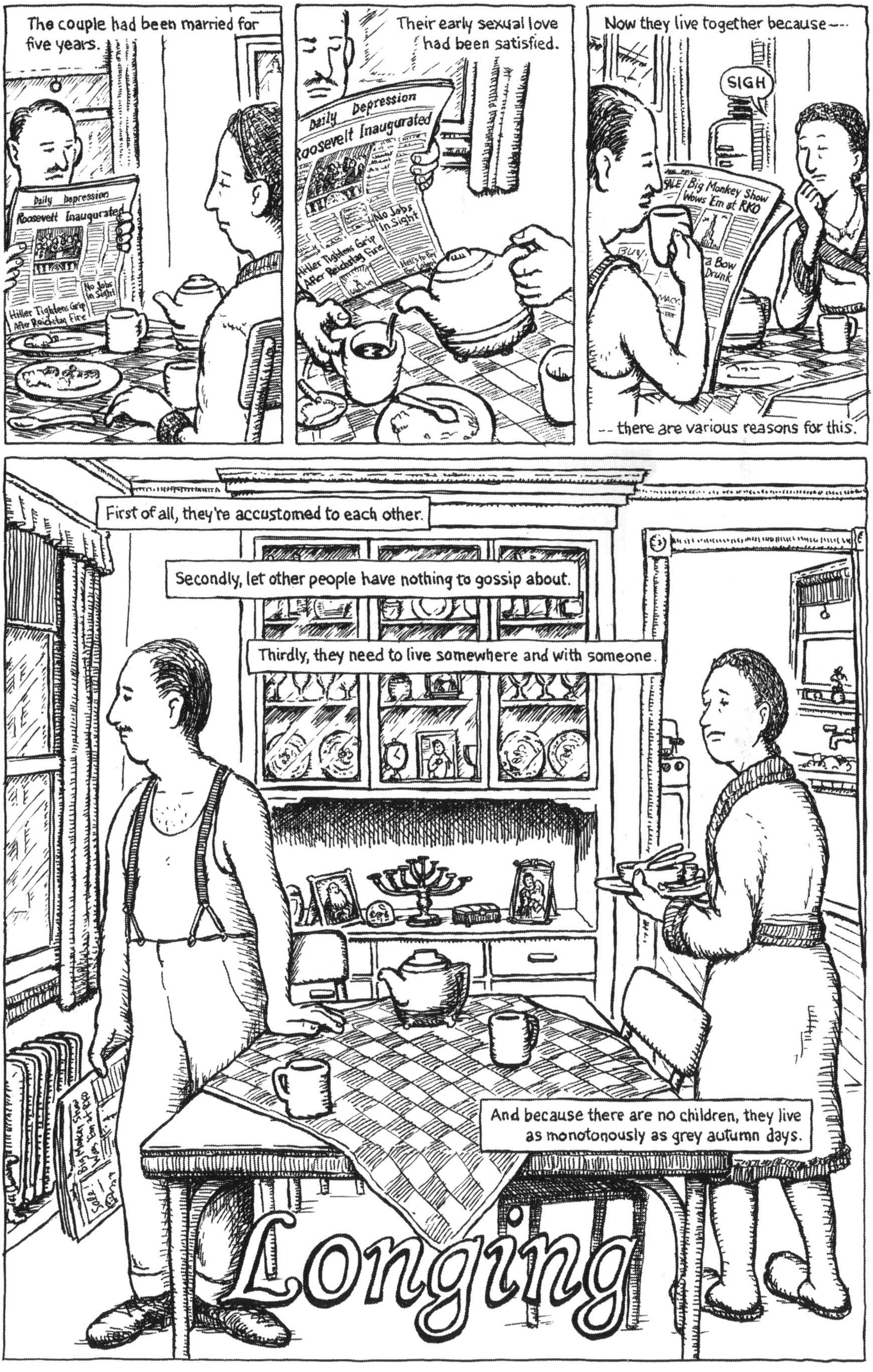
The couple had been married for five years.
Daily Depression
Roosevelt Inaugurated
No Jobs In Sight
Hitler Tightens Grip After Reichstag Fire
Their early sexual love had been satisfied.
Daily Depression
Roosevelt Inaugurated
No Jobs In Sight
Hitler Tightens Grip After Reichstag Fire
Now they live together because---
SIGH
Big Monkey Show Wows Em at RKO
-- there are various reasons for this.
First of all, they're accustomed to each other.
Secondly, let other people have nothing to gossip about.
Thirdly, they need to live somewhere and with someone.
And because there are no children, they live as monotonously as grey autumn days.
Longing

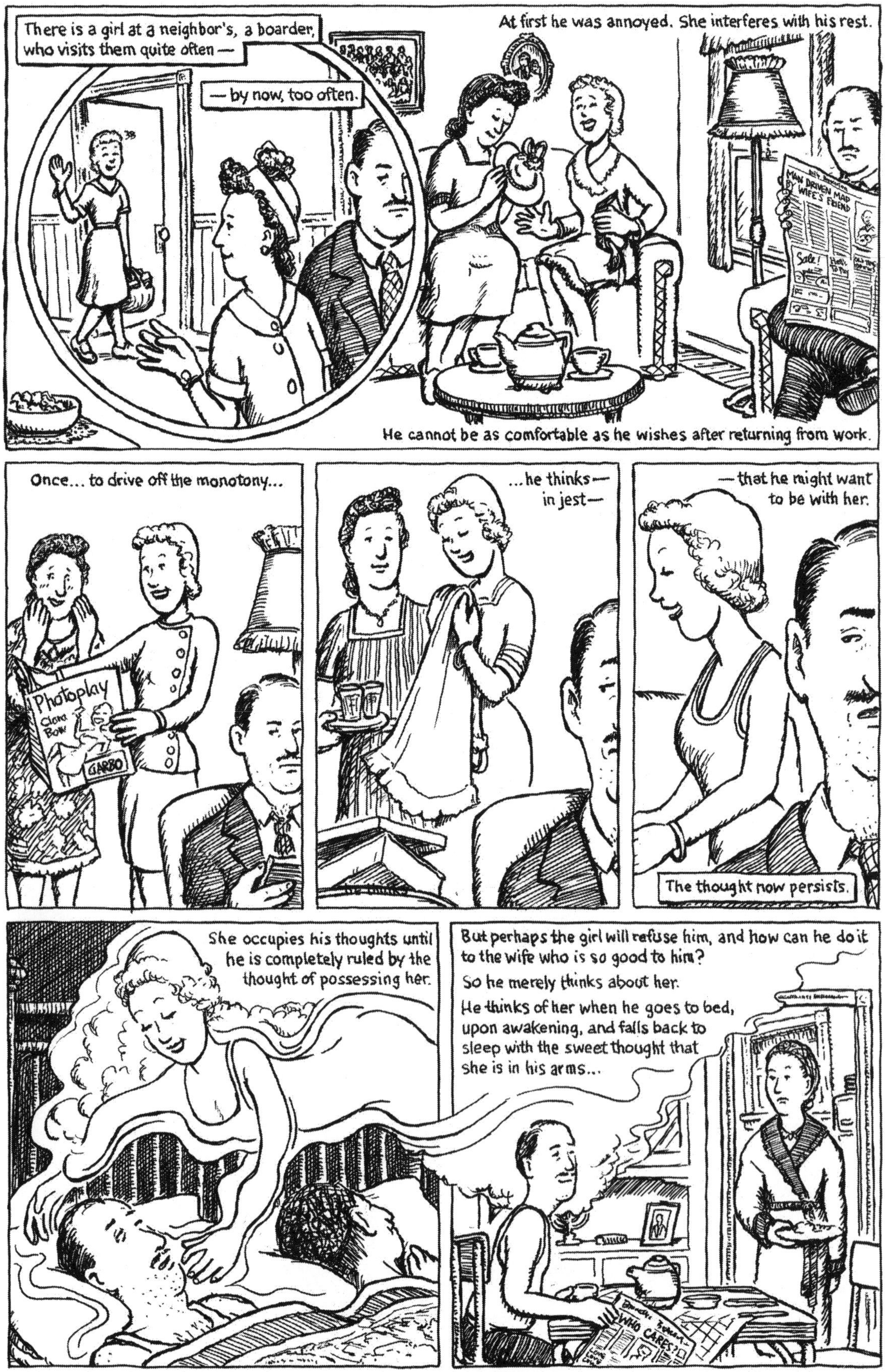
There is a girl at a neighbor's, a boarder, who visits them quite often —
— by now, too often.
At first he was annoyed. She interferes with his rest.
MAN DRIVEN MAD BY WIFE'S FRIEND
Sale!
He cannot be as comfortable as he wishes after returning from work.
Once... to drive off the monotony...
Photoplay
Clara Bow
GARBO
...he thinks — in jest —
— that he might want to be with her.
The thought now persists.
She occupies his thoughts until he is completely ruled by the thought of possessing her.
But perhaps the girl will refuse him, and how can he do it to the wife who is so good to him?
So he merely thinks about her.
He thinks of her when he goes to bed, upon awakening, and falls back to sleep with the sweet thought that she is in his arms...
WHO CARES?

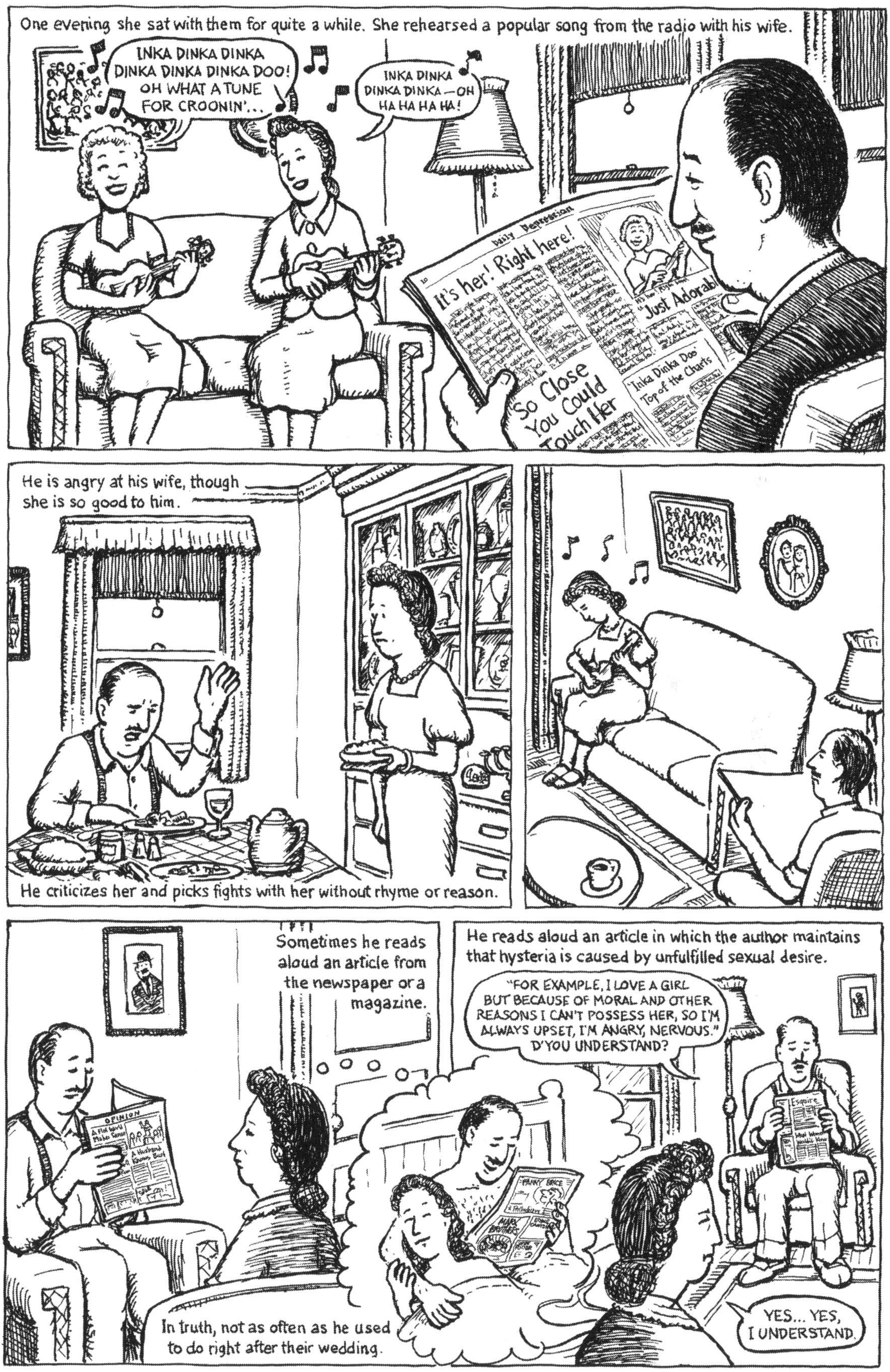

One evening she sat with them for quite a while. She rehearsed a popular song from the radio with his wife.
INKA DINKA DINKA DINKA DINKA DINKA DOO! OH WHAT A TUNE FOR CROONIN'...
INKA DINKA DINKA DINKA—OH HA HA HA HA!
Daily Depression
It's her! Right here!
Just Adorabl
So Close You Could Touch Her
'Inka Dinka Doo' Top of the Charts
He is angry at his wife, though she is so good to him.
He criticizes her and picks fights with her without rhyme or reason.
Sometimes he reads aloud an article from the newspaper or a magazine.
OPINION
In truth, not as often as he used to do right after their wedding.
FANNY BRICE
MARX BROTHERS
He reads aloud an article in which the author maintains that hysteria is caused by unfulfilled sexual desire.
"FOR EXAMPLE, I LOVE A GIRL BUT BECAUSE OF MORAL AND OTHER REASONS I CAN'T POSSESS HER, SO I'M ALWAYS UPSET, I'M ANGRY, NERVOUS." D'YOU UNDERSTAND?
Esquire
YES... YES, I UNDERSTAND.

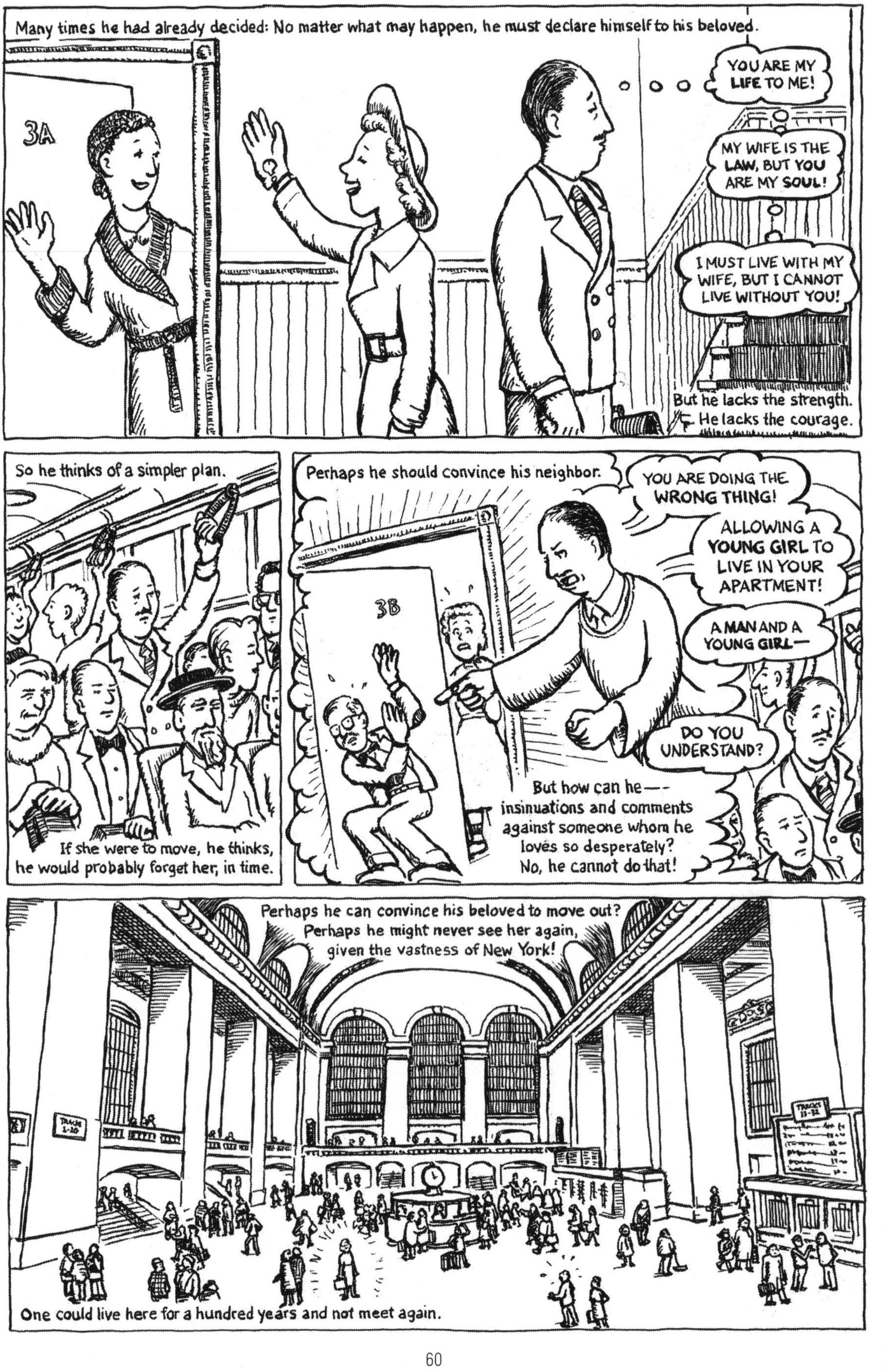
Many times he had already decided: No matter what may happen, he must declare himself to his beloved.
3A
YOU ARE MY LIFE TO ME!
MY WIFE IS THE LAW, BUT YOU ARE MY SOUL!
I MUST LIVE WITH MY WIFE, BUT I CANNOT LIVE WITHOUT YOU!
But he lacks the strength. He lacks the courage.
So he thinks of a simpler plan.
If she were to move, he thinks, he would probably forget her, in time.
Perhaps he should convince his neighbor.
YOU ARE DOING THE WRONG THING!
ALLOWING A YOUNG GIRL TO LIVE IN YOUR APARTMENT!
A MAN AND A YOUNG GIRL—
3B
DO YOU UNDERSTAND?
But how can he— insinuations and comments against someone whom he loves so desperately? No, he cannot do that!
Perhaps he can convince his beloved to move out? Perhaps he might never see her again, given the vastness of New York!
One could live here for a hundred years and not meet again.

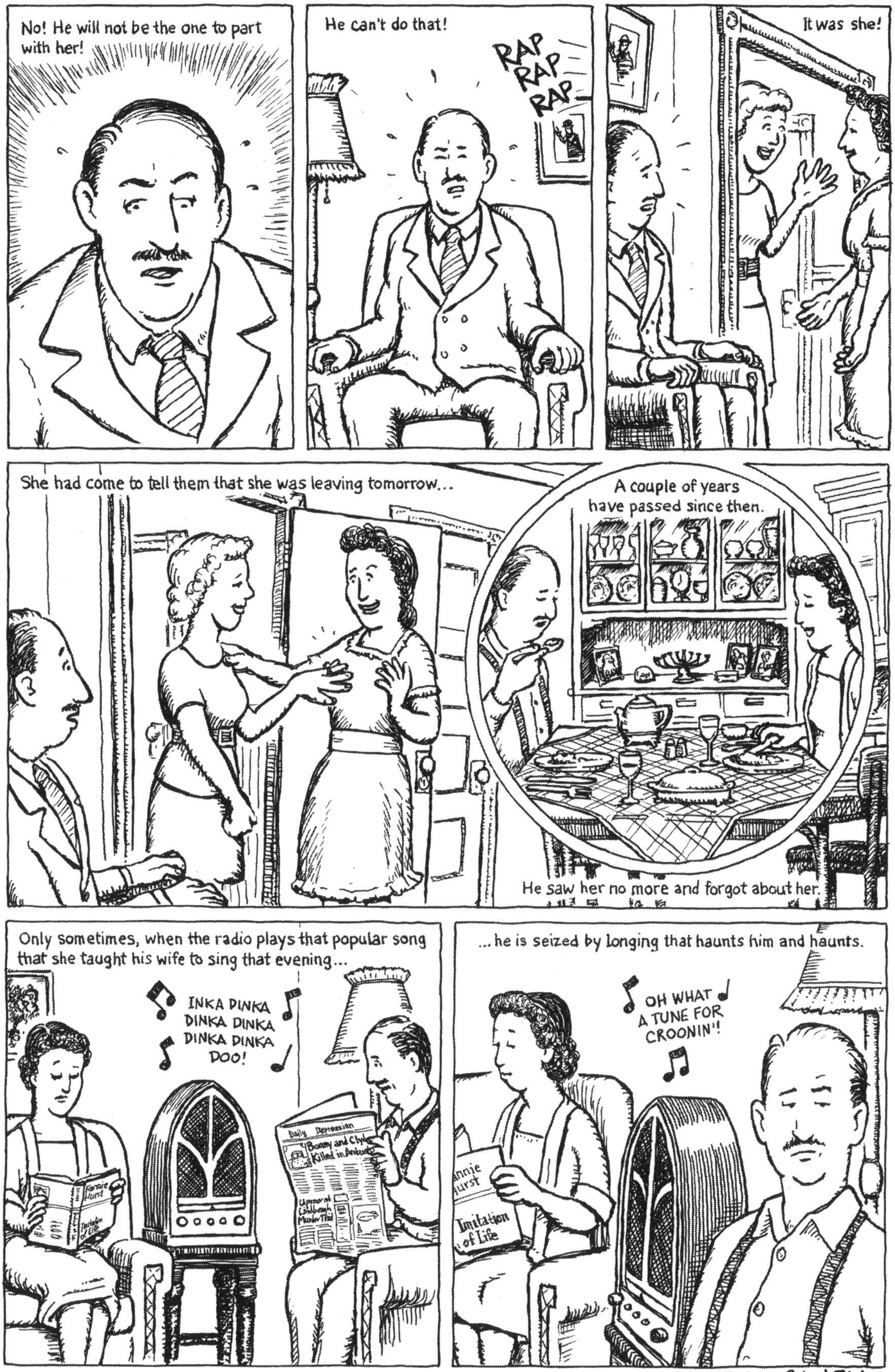
No! He will not be the one to part with her!
He can't do that!
RAP RAP RAP
It was she!
She had come to tell them that she was leaving tomorrow...
A couple of years have passed since then.
He saw her no more and forgot about her.
Only sometimes, when the radio plays that popular song that she taught his wife to sing that evening...
INKA DINKA DINKA DINKA DINKA DINKA DOO!
Daily Depression
...he is seized by longing that haunts him and haunts.
OH WHAT A TUNE FOR CROONIN'!
Imitation of Life

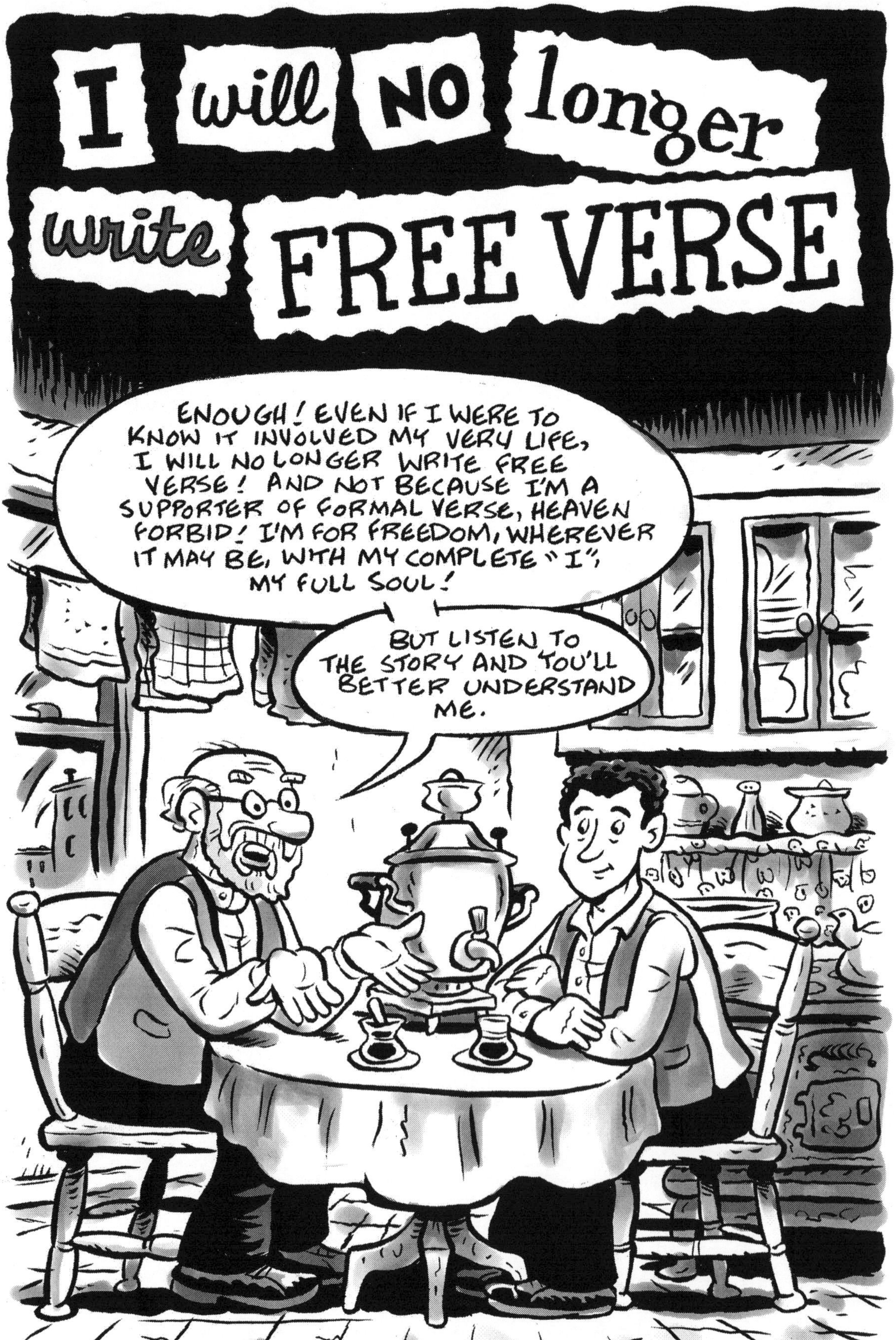
I will NO longer write FREE VERSE
ENOUGH! EVEN IF I WERE TO KNOW IT INVOLVED MY VERY LIFE, I WILL NO LONGER WRITE FREE VERSE! AND NOT BECAUSE I'M A SUPPORTER OF FORMAL VERSE, HEAVEN FORBID! I'M FOR FREEDOM, WHEREVER IT MAY BE, WITH MY COMPLETE "I", MY FULL SOUL!
BUT LISTEN TO THE STORY AND YOU'LL BETTER UNDERSTAND ME.
T. LABAN 2016

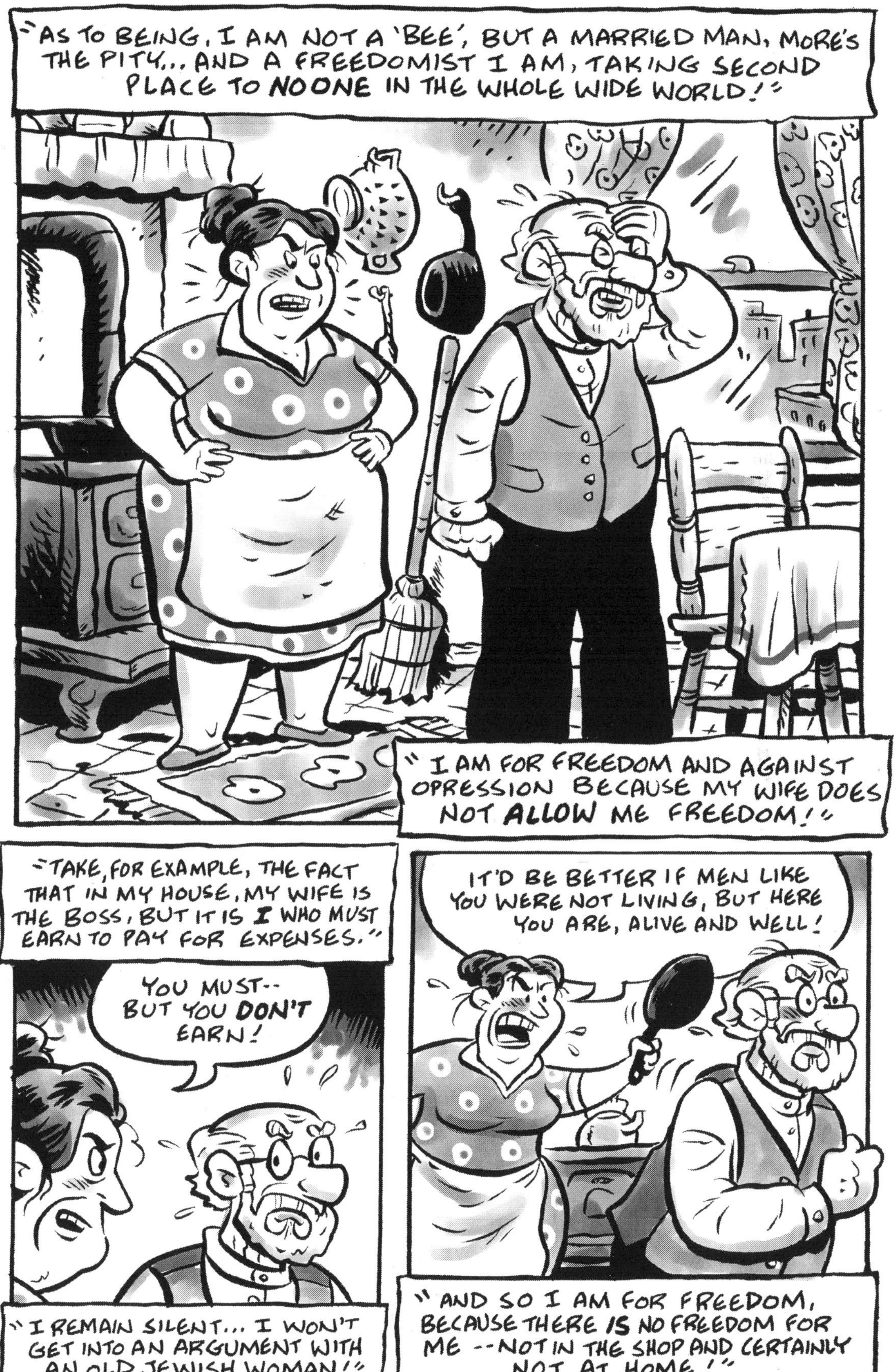
"AS TO BEING, I AM NOT A 'BEE', BUT A MARRIED MAN, MORE'S THE PITY... AND A FREEDOMIST I AM, TAKING SECOND PLACE TO **NO ONE** IN THE WHOLE WIDE WORLD!"
"I AM FOR FREEDOM AND AGAINST OPRESSION BECAUSE MY WIFE DOES NOT **ALLOW** ME FREEDOM!"
"TAKE, FOR EXAMPLE, THE FACT THAT IN MY HOUSE, MY WIFE IS THE BOSS, BUT IT IS **I** WHO MUST EARN TO PAY FOR EXPENSES."
YOU MUST-- BUT YOU **DON'T** EARN!
"I REMAIN SILENT... I WON'T GET INTO AN ARGUMENT WITH AN OLD JEWISH WOMAN!"
IT'D BE BETTER IF MEN LIKE YOU WERE NOT LIVING, BUT HERE YOU ARE, ALIVE AND WELL!
"AND SO I AM FOR FREEDOM, BECAUSE THERE **IS** NO FREEDOM FOR ME --NOT IN THE SHOP AND CERTAINLY NOT AT HOME!"

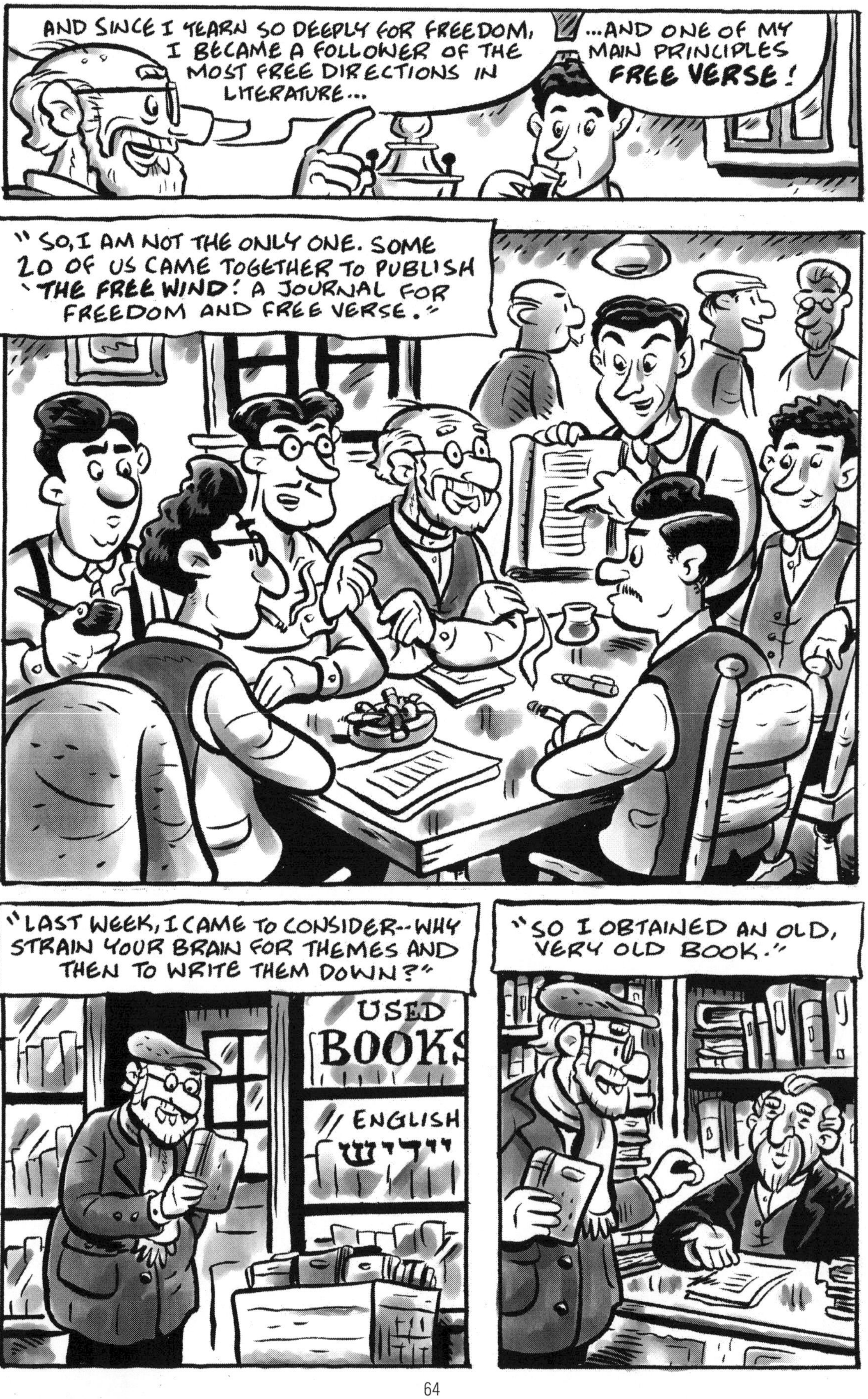
AND SINCE I YEARN SO DEEPLY FOR FREEDOM, I BECAME A FOLLOWER OF THE MOST FREE DIRECTIONS IN LITERATURE...
...AND ONE OF MY MAIN PRINCIPLES **FREE VERSE!**
"SO, I AM NOT THE ONLY ONE. SOME 20 OF US CAME TOGETHER TO PUBLISH '**THE FREE WIND**': A JOURNAL FOR FREEDOM AND FREE VERSE."
"LAST WEEK, I CAME TO CONSIDER--WHY STRAIN YOUR BRAIN FOR THEMES AND THEN TO WRITE THEM DOWN?"
USED
BOOKS
ENGLISH
יידיש
"SO I OBTAINED AN OLD, VERY OLD BOOK."

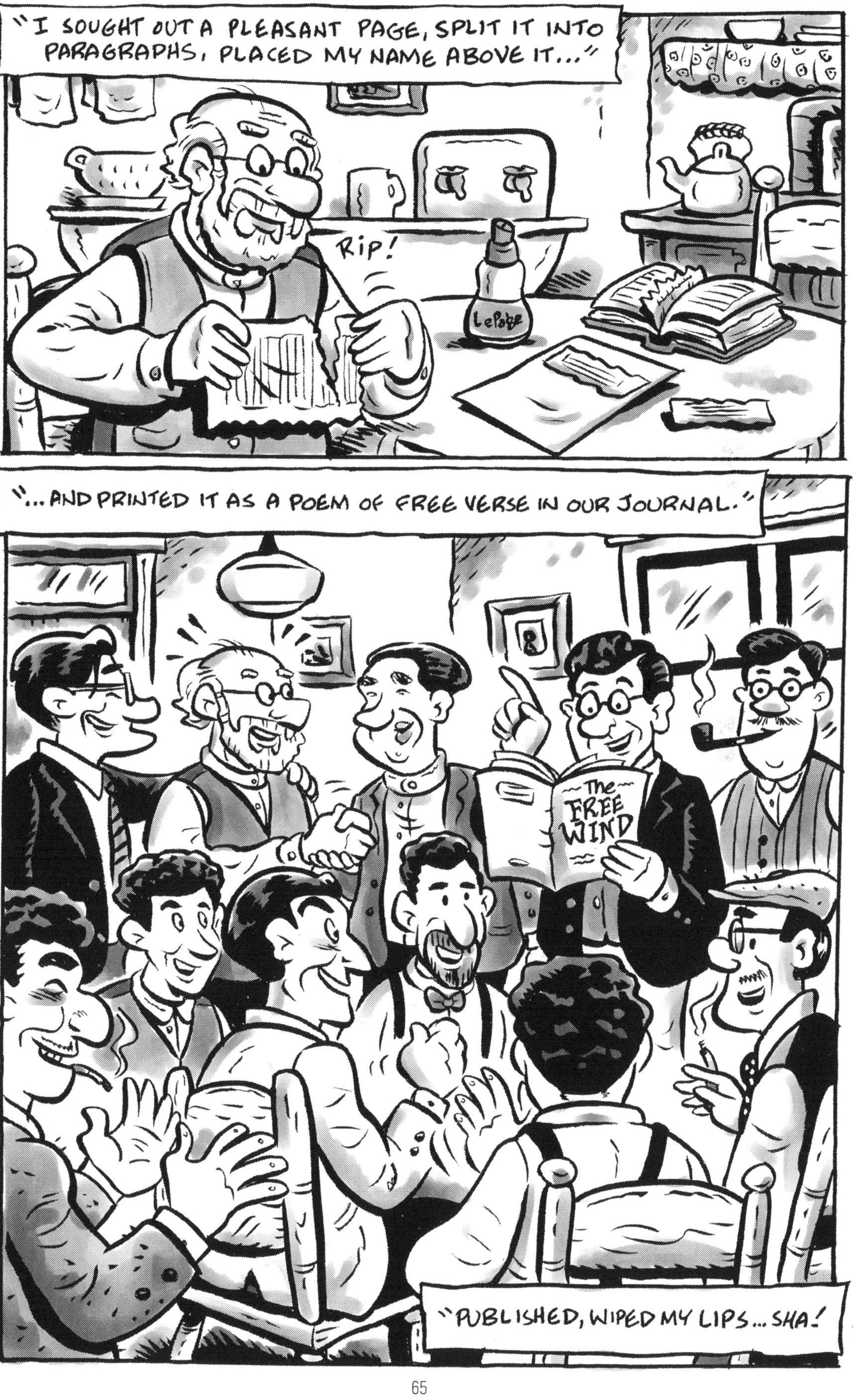
"I SOUGHT OUT A PLEASANT PAGE, SPLIT IT INTO PARAGRAPHS, PLACED MY NAME ABOVE IT..."
RIP!
LePage
"...AND PRINTED IT AS A POEM OF FREE VERSE IN OUR JOURNAL."
The FREE WIND
"PUBLISHED, WIPED MY LIPS... SHA!"

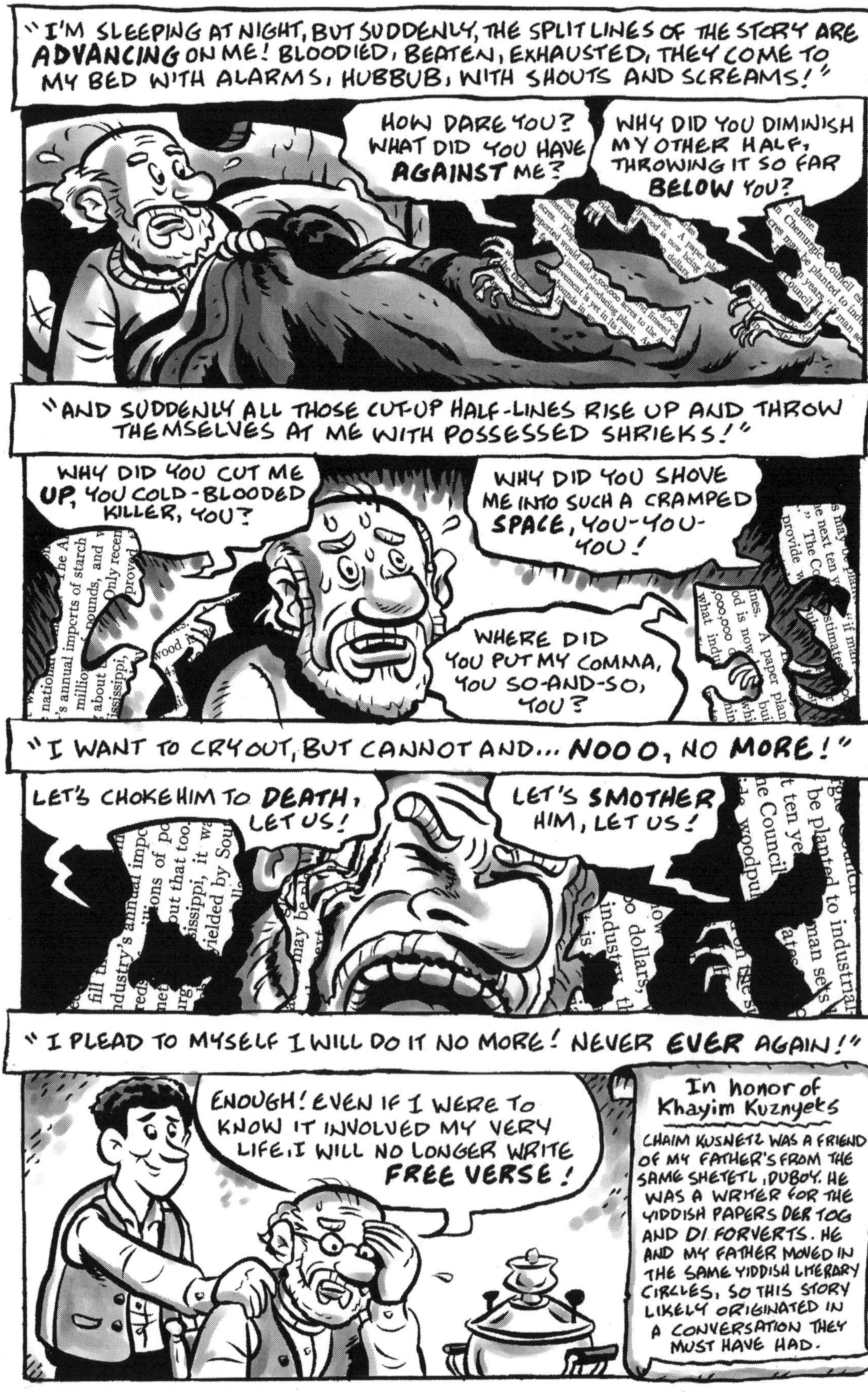
"I'M SLEEPING AT NIGHT, BUT SUDDENLY, THE SPLIT LINES OF THE STORY ARE ADVANCING ON ME! BLOODIED, BEATEN, EXHAUSTED, THEY COME TO MY BED WITH ALARMS, HUBBUB, WITH SHOUTS AND SCREAMS!"
HOW DARE YOU? WHAT DID YOU HAVE AGAINST ME?
WHY DID YOU DIMINISH MY OTHER HALF, THROWING IT SO FAR BELOW YOU?
"AND SUDDENLY ALL THOSE CUT-UP HALF-LINES RISE UP AND THROW THEMSELVES AT ME WITH POSSESSED SHRIEKS!"
WHY DID YOU CUT ME UP, YOU COLD-BLOODED KILLER, YOU?
WHY DID YOU SHOVE ME INTO SUCH A CRAMPED SPACE, YOU-YOU-YOU!
WHERE DID YOU PUT MY COMMA, YOU SO-AND-SO, YOU?
"I WANT TO CRY OUT, BUT CANNOT AND... NOOO, NO MORE!"
LET'S CHOKE HIM TO DEATH, LET US!
LET'S SMOTHER HIM, LET US!
"I PLEAD TO MYSELF I WILL DO IT NO MORE! NEVER EVER AGAIN!"
ENOUGH! EVEN IF I WERE TO KNOW IT INVOLVED MY VERY LIFE, I WILL NO LONGER WRITE FREE VERSE!
In honor of Khayim Kuznyets
CHAIM KUSNETZ WAS A FRIEND OF MY FATHER'S FROM THE SAME SHETETL, DUBOY. HE WAS A WRITER FOR THE YIDDISH PAPERS DER TOG AND DI FORVERTS. HE AND MY FATHER MOVED IN THE SAME YIDDISH LITERARY CIRCLES, SO THIS STORY LIKELY ORIGINATED IN A CONVERSATION THEY MUST HAVE HAD.

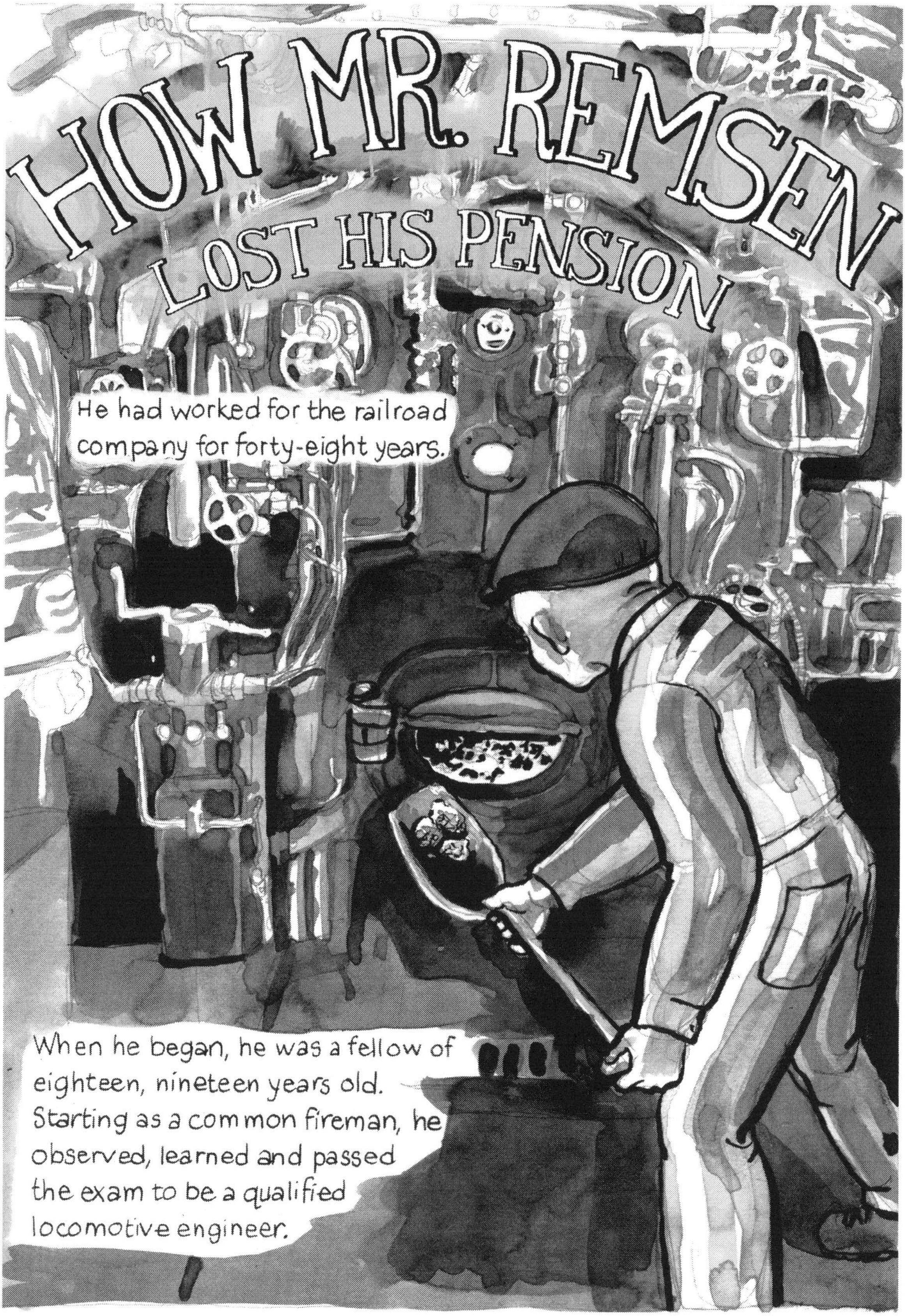
HOW MR. REMSEN LOST HIS PENSION
He had worked for the railroad company for forty-eight years.
When he began, he was a fellow of eighteen, nineteen years old. Starting as a common fireman, he observed, learned and passed the exam to be a qualified locomotive engineer.

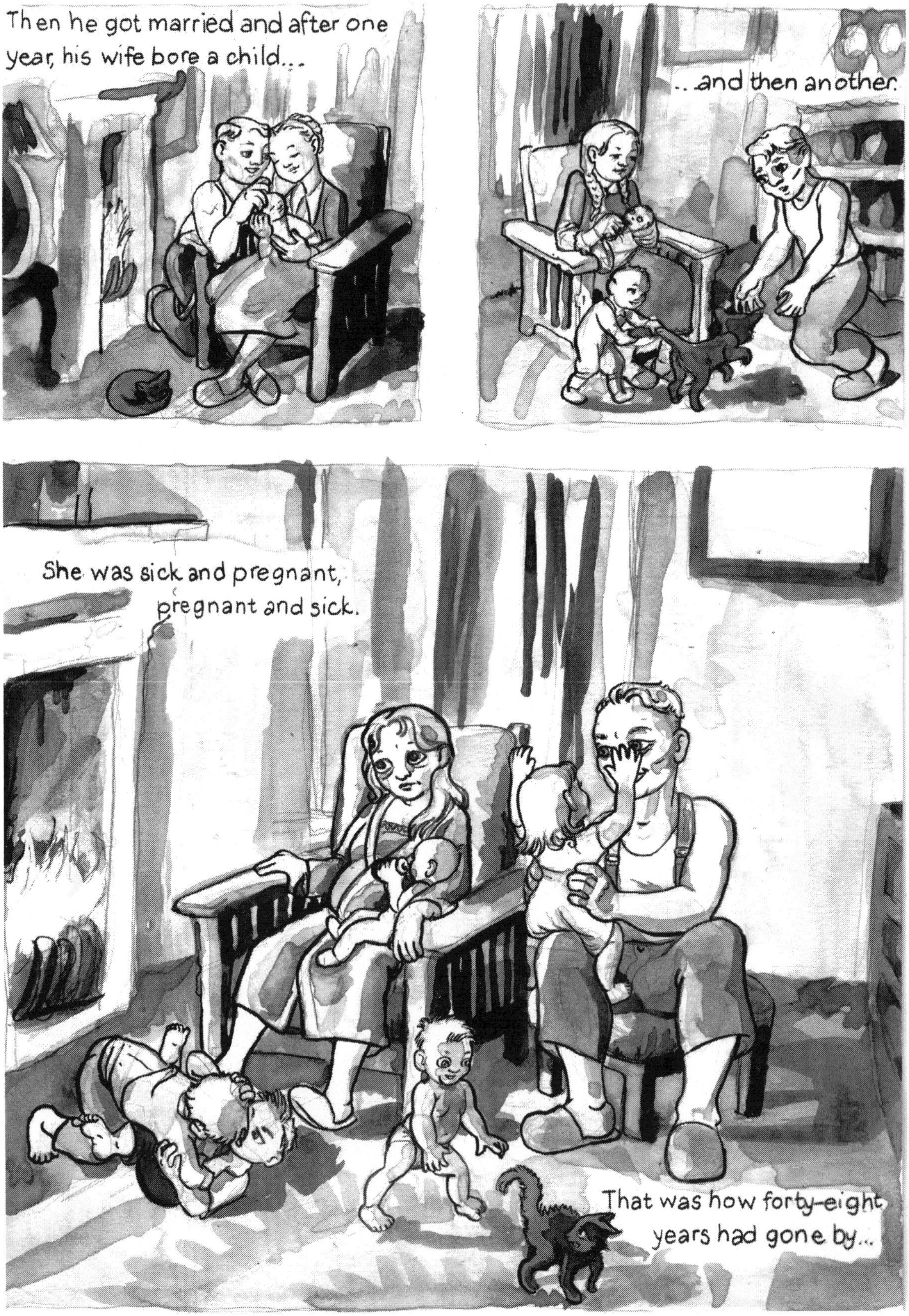
Then he got married and after one year, his wife bore a child...
...and then another.
She was sick and pregnant, pregnant and sick.
That was how forty-eight years had gone by...

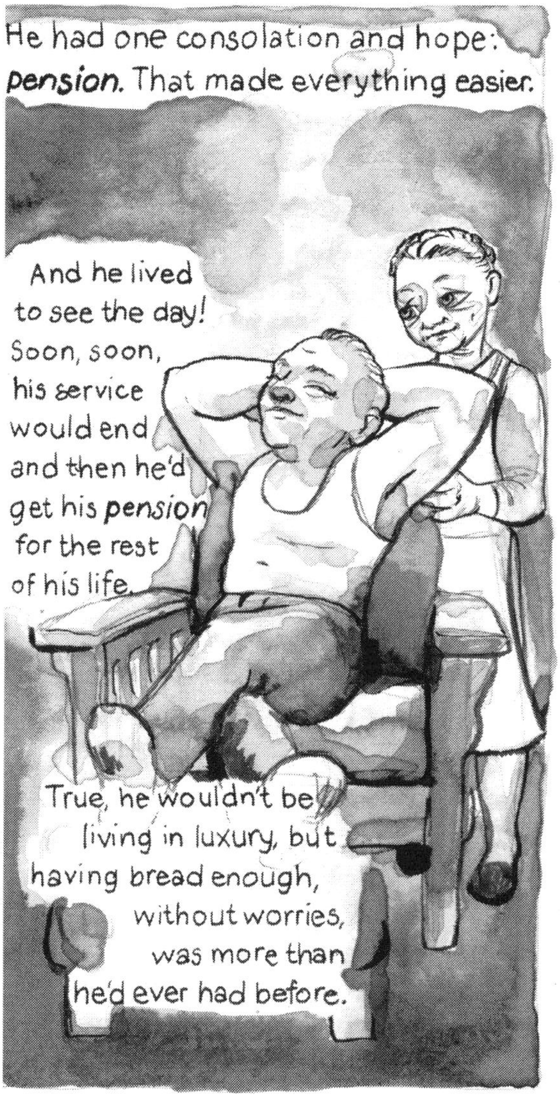
He had one consolation and hope: **pension.** That made everything easier.
And he lived to see the day! Soon, soon, his service would end and then he'd get his **pension** for the rest of his life.
True, he wouldn't be living in luxury, but having bread enough, without worries, was more than he'd ever had before.

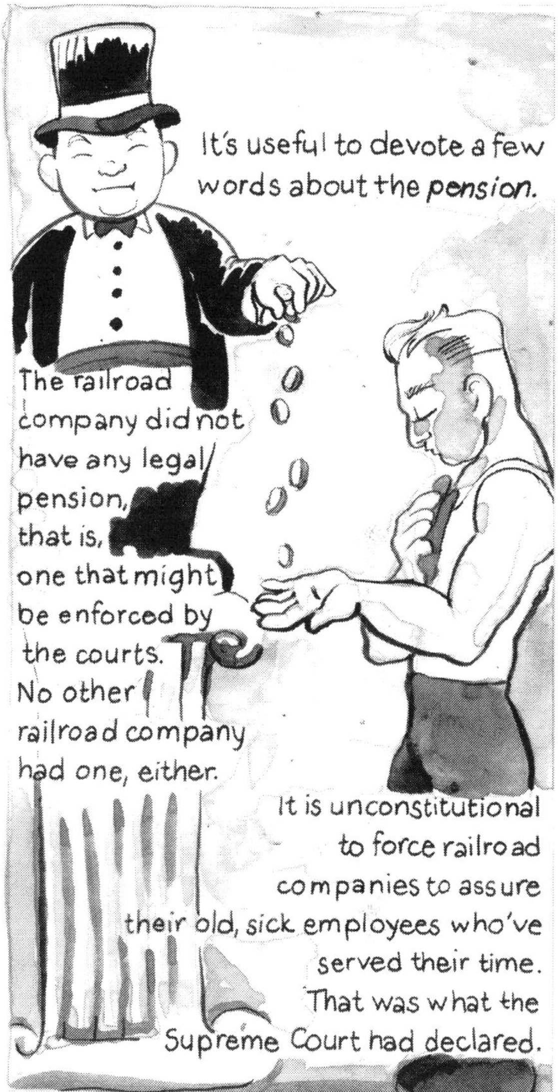
It's useful to devote a few words about the **pension.**
The railroad company did not have any legal pension, that is, one that might be enforced by the courts. No other railroad company had one, either.
It is unconstitutional to force railroad companies to assure their old, sick employees who've served their time. That was what the Supreme Court had declared.

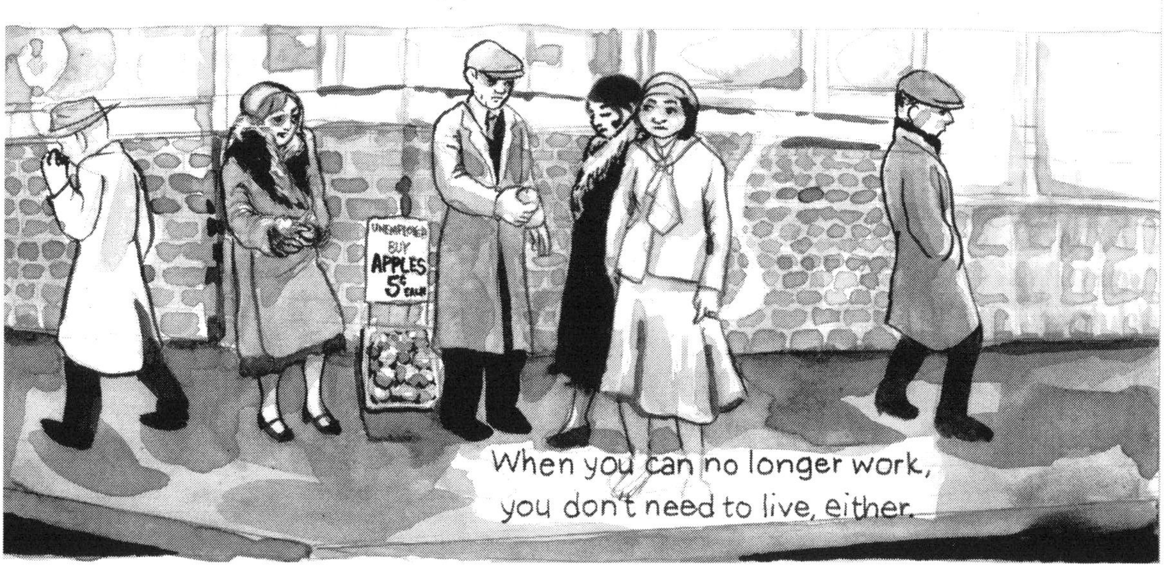
BUY APPLES 5¢
When you can no longer work, you don't need to live, either.

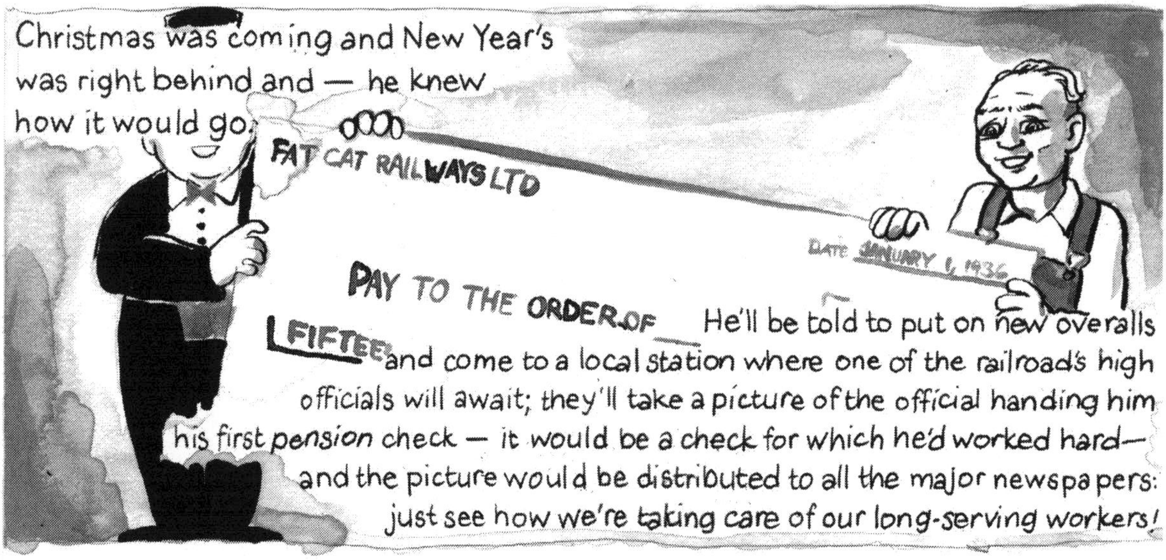
Christmas was coming and New Year's was right behind and — he knew how it would go.
FAT CAT RAILWAYS LTD
DATE JANUARY 1, 1936
PAY TO THE ORDER OF
FIFTEE
He'll be told to put on new overalls and come to a local station where one of the railroad's high officials will await; they'll take a picture of the official handing him his first *pension* check — it would be a check for which he'd worked hard— and the picture would be distributed to all the major newspapers: just see how we're taking care of our long-serving workers!

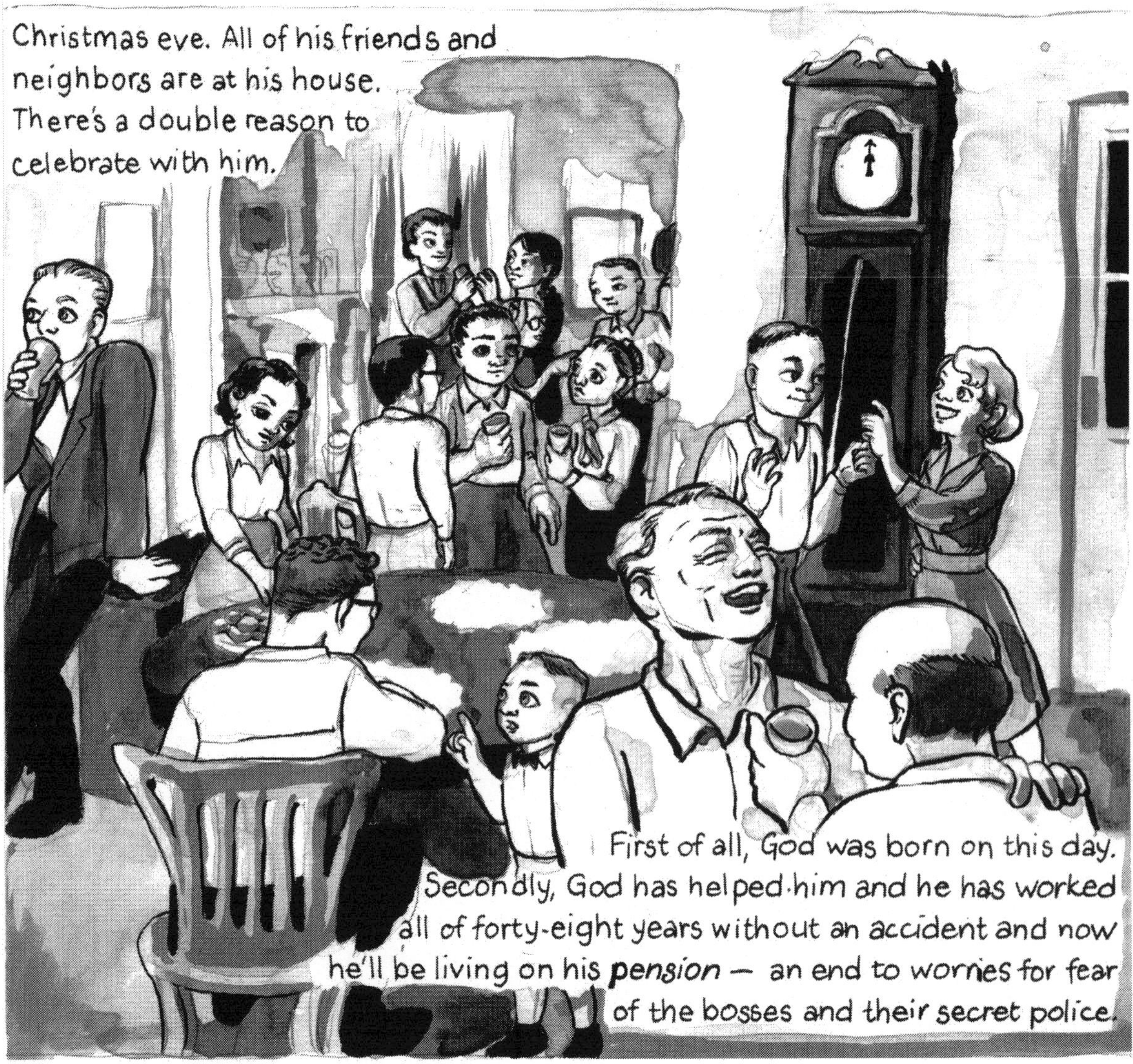
Christmas eve. All of his friends and neighbors are at his house. There's a double reason to celebrate with him.
First of all, God was born on this day. Secondly, God has helped him and he has worked all of forty-eight years without an accident and now he'll be living on his ***pension*** — an end to worries for fear of the bosses and their secret police.

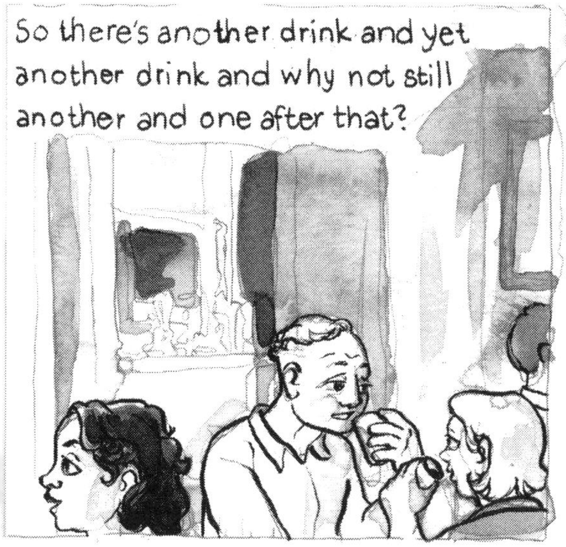
So there's another drink and yet another drink and why not still another and one after that?

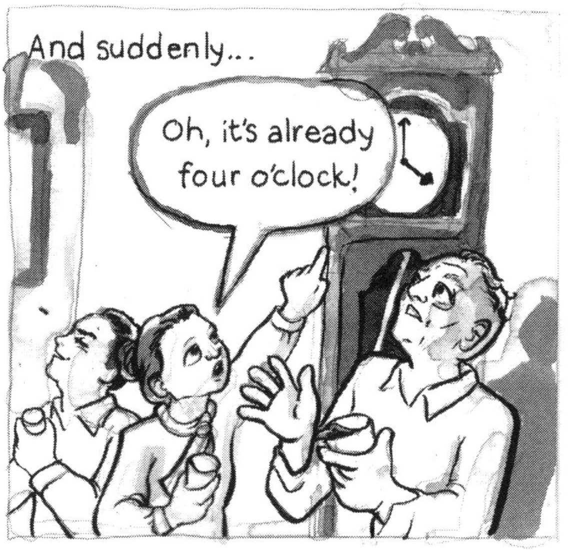
And suddenly...
Oh, it's already four o'clock!

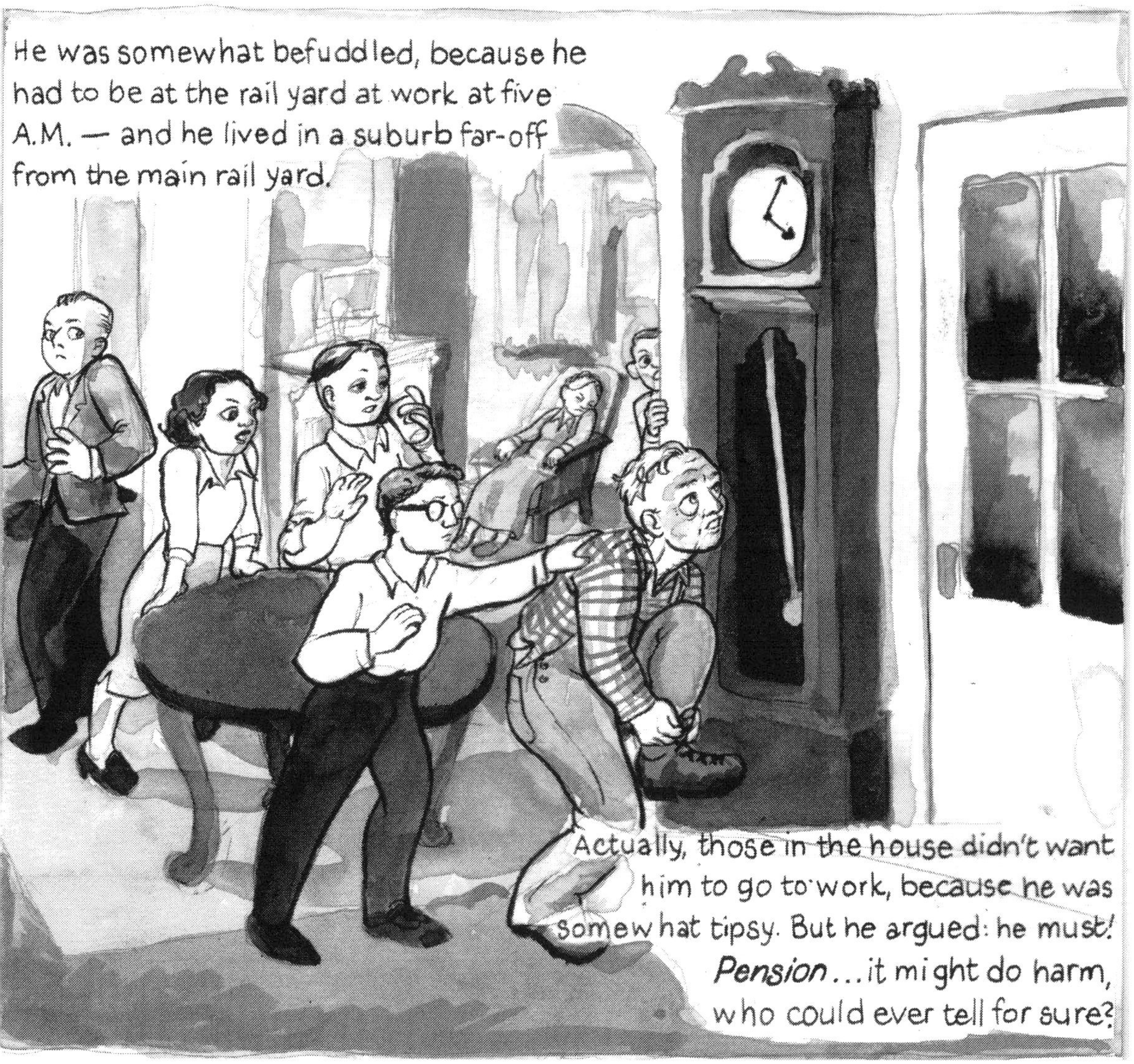
He was somewhat befuddled, because he had to be at the rail yard at work at five A.M. — and he lived in a suburb far-off from the main rail yard.
Actually, those in the house didn't want him to go to work, because he was somewhat tipsy. But he argued: he must! *Pension*... it might do harm, who could ever tell for sure?

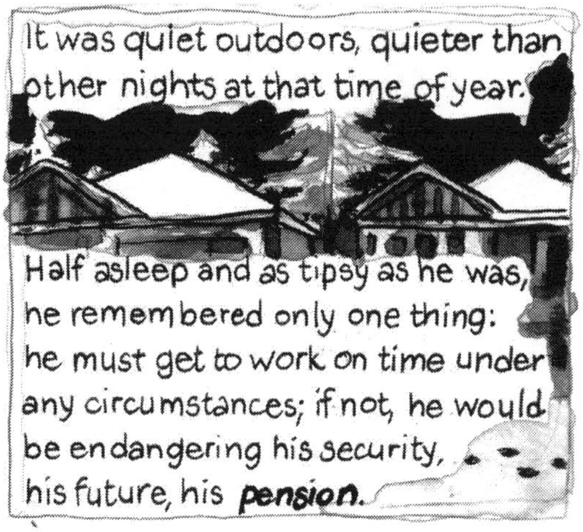
It was quiet outdoors, quieter than other nights at that time of year.
Half asleep and as tipsy as he was, he remembered only one thing: he must get to work on time under any circumstances; if not, he would be endangering his security, his future, his **pension.**

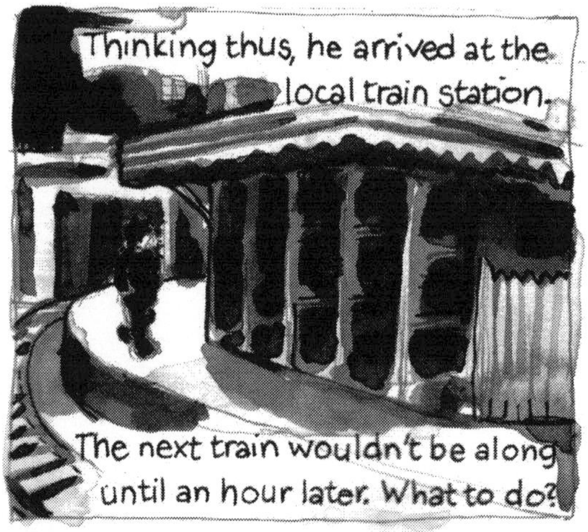
Thinking thus, he arrived at the local train station.
The next train wouldn't be along until an hour later. What to do?

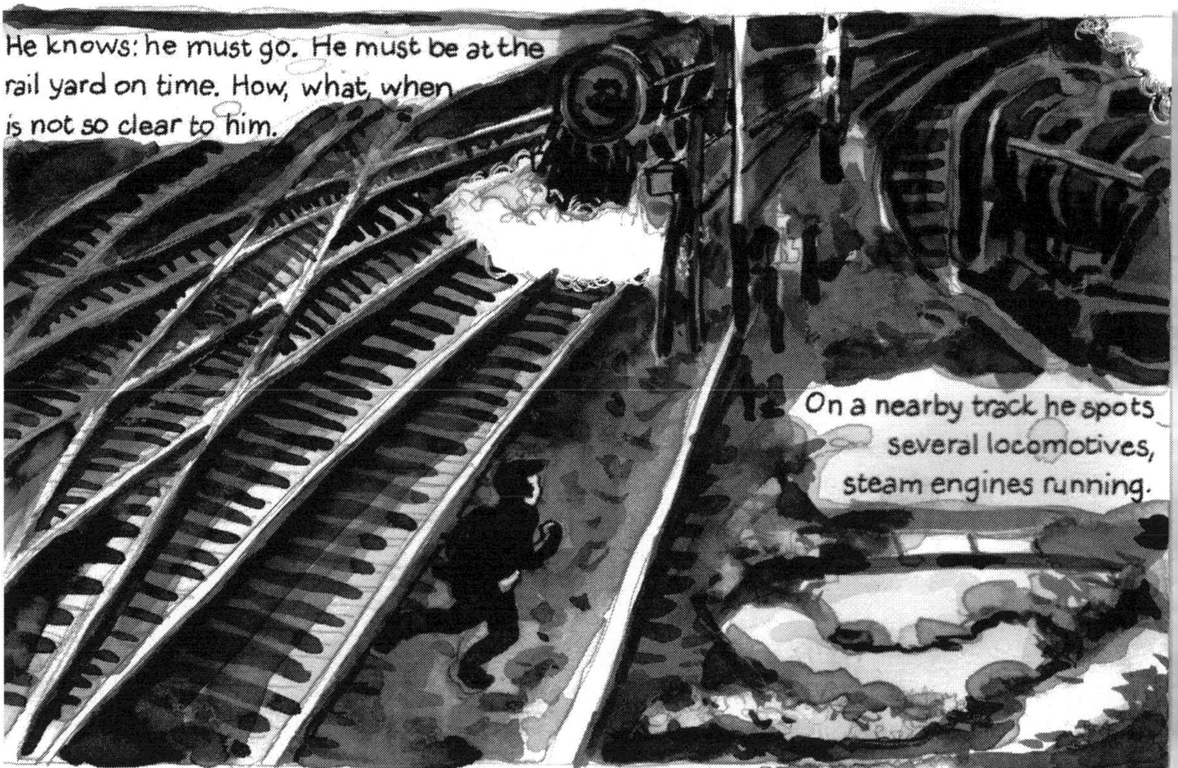
He knows: he must go. He must be at the rail yard on time. How, what, when is not so clear to him.
On a nearby track he spots several locomotives, steam engines running.

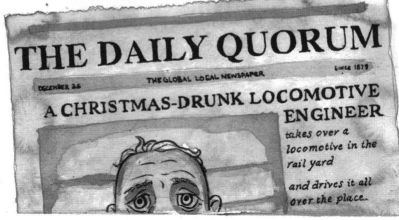

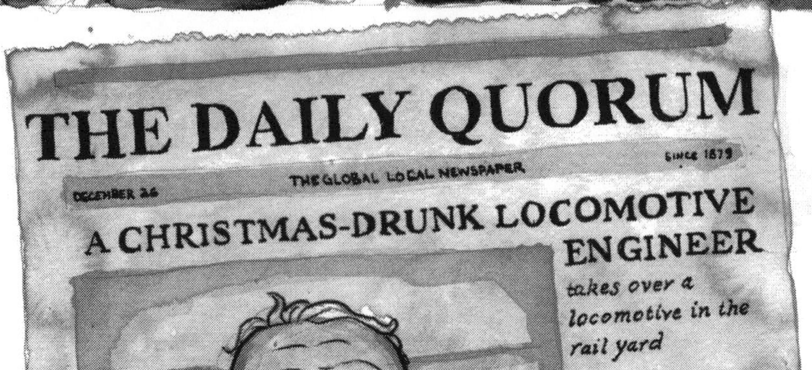
THE DAILY QUORUM
SINCE 1879
DECEMBER 26
THE GLOBAL LOCAL NEWSPAPER
A CHRISTMAS-DRUNK LOCOMOTIVE ENGINEER
takes over a locomotive in the rail yard
and drives it all over the place.

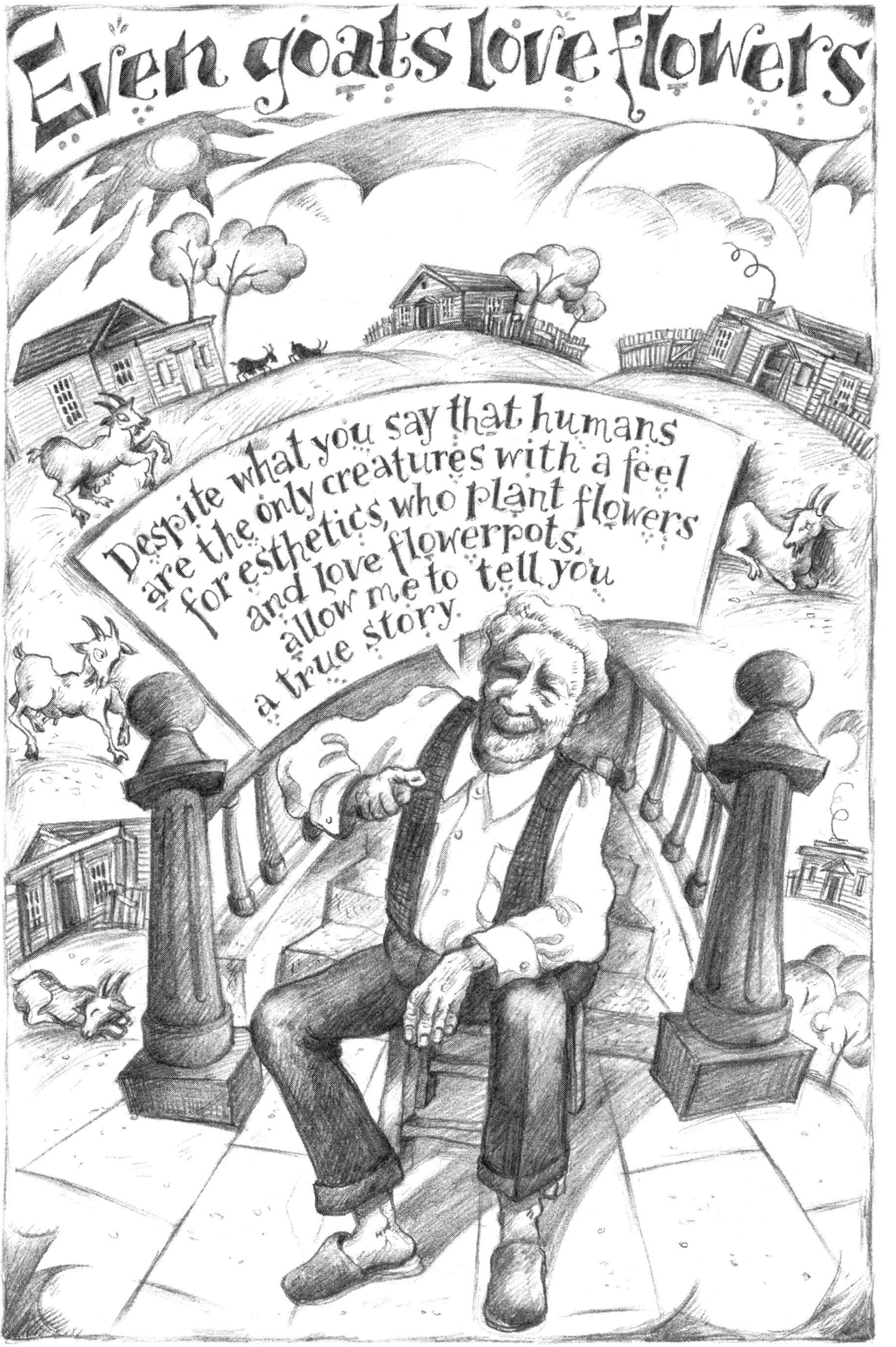
Even goats love flowers
Despite what you say that humans
are the only creatures with a feel
for esthetics, who plant flowers
and love flowerpots,
allow me to tell you
a true story.

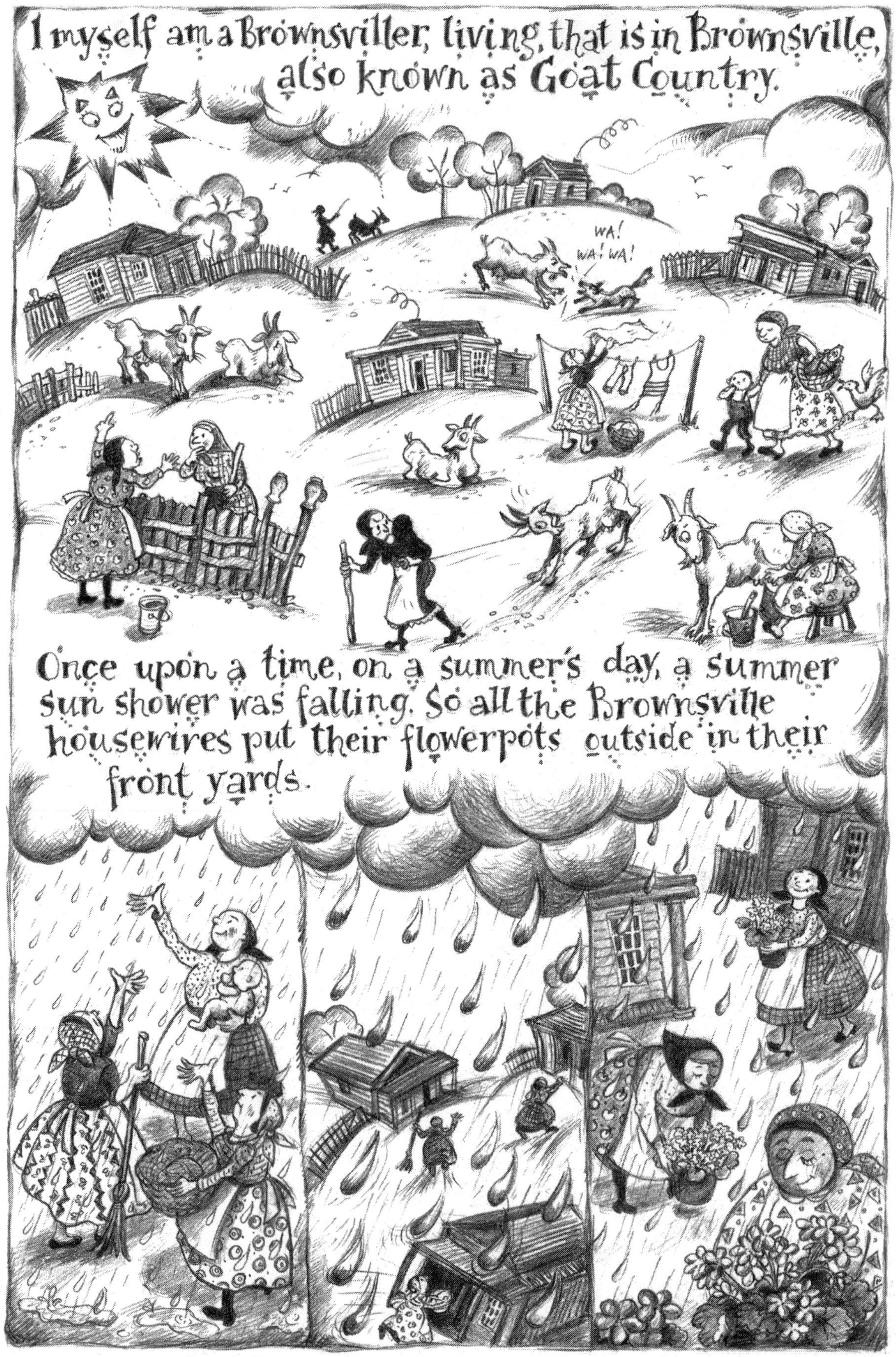
I myself am a Brownsviller, living, that is in Brownsville, also known as Goat Country.
WA! WA! WA!
Once upon a time, on a summer's day, a summer sun shower was falling. So all the Brownsville housewives put their flowerpots outside in their front yards.

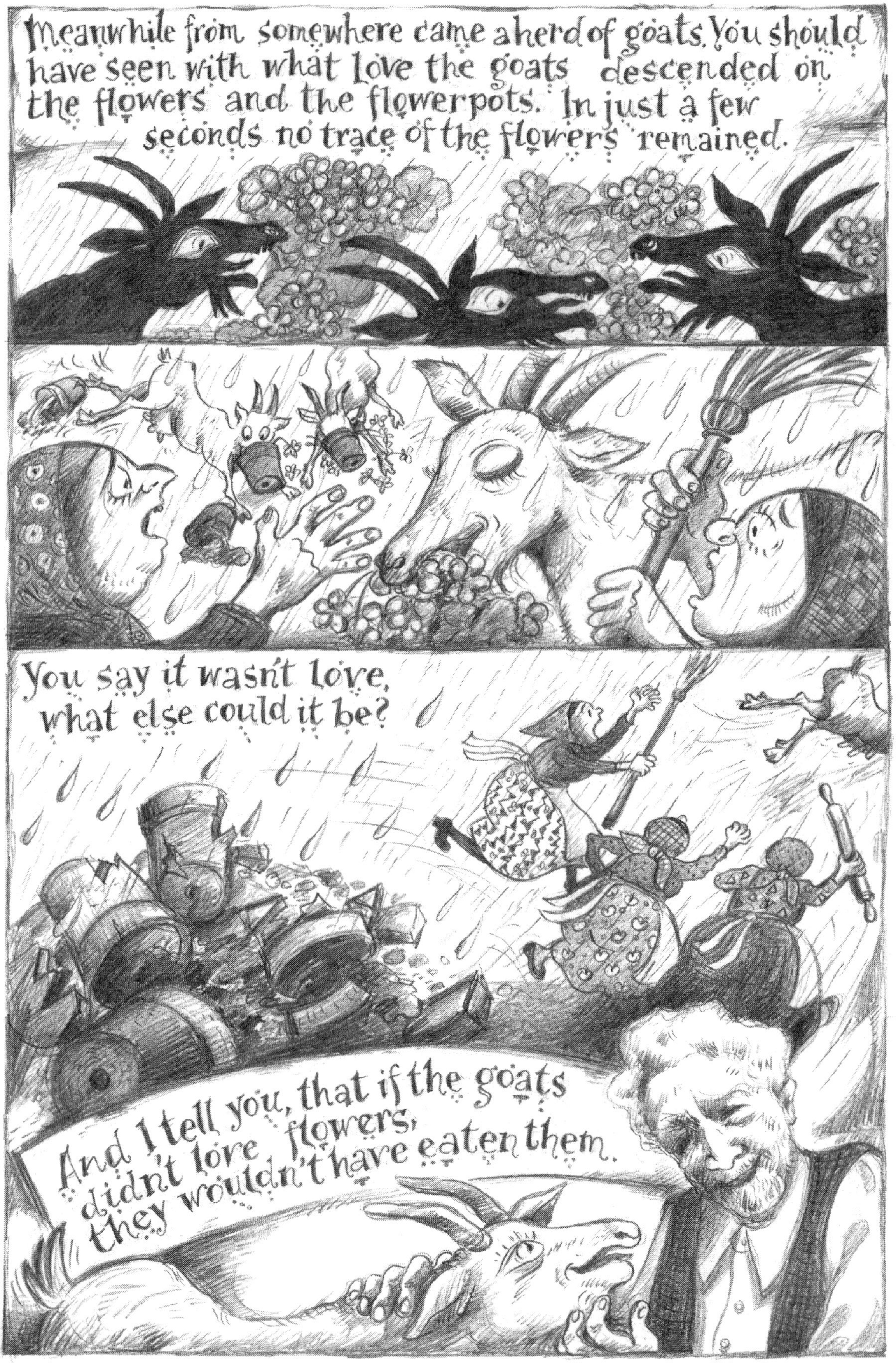
Meanwhile from somewhere came a herd of goats. You should have seen with what love the goats descended on the flowers and the flowerpots. In just a few seconds no trace of the flowers remained.
You say it wasn't love, what else could it be?
And I tell you, that if the goats didn't love flowers, they wouldn't have eaten them.

A SHORT GLOSSARY

A brief history of Yiddish Yiddish is a fusion language, composed of Medieval Germanic dialects, Hebrew-Aramaic, Slavic, and Romance (Latin-based) languages (Old French and Old Italian). Early Jewish languages that led up to Yiddish were Hebrew (until 586 BC), Judeo-Aramaic (500–200 BC), Judeo-Greek (4th Century BC) and Judeo-Latin (63 BC–70 AD). It arose in the German Rhineland around 900-1050 AD when Romance language-speaking Jews began to settle in the German-speaking Rhineland, combining Romance and Germanic languages. In 1098, the Jewish people were expelled from Bohemia (Southeastern German) into Poland by Crusaders, bringing contact with Slavic languages, and thus was formed Yiddish.

Pentateuch The first five books of the Hebrew scriptures

Reb A term of respect, like Mister, Senor, Monsieur

Shabes Shabes is the Sabbath, Saturday

Shul Synagogue, temple

Simkhes Toyre A Jewish holiday that celebrates and marks the conclusion of the annual cycle of public Torah readings, and the beginning of a new cycle. This is the only time of year on which the Torah scrolls are taken out of the ark and read at night and in the morning.

On each occasion, when the ark is opened, the worshippers leave their seats to dance and sing with the Torah scrolls in a joyous celebration that can last for several hours.

(Thanks to Wikipedia)

Zayde Grandfather

Chaim Kuznets (page 66) More about Chaim Kuznets can be found in the book, "My Future is in America," an anthology of Jewish immigrant auto-biographies, published by New York University Press. Both Chaim and his wife Minnie have chapters in the book.

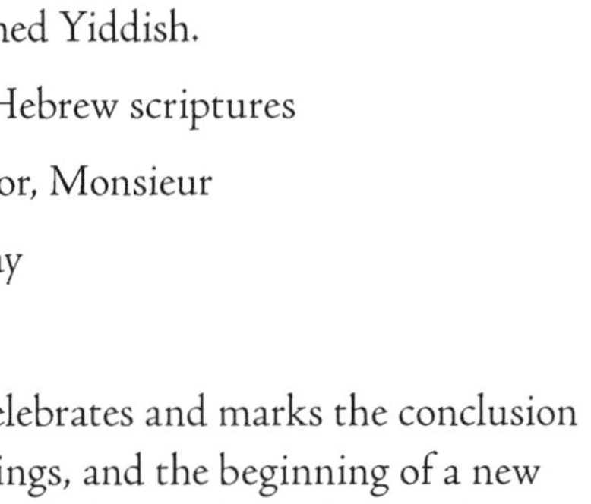

Left to right: Mutye in a bow tie, unidenti-fied friend, and Chaim.

ARTIST BIOS

BARBARA 'WILLY' MENDES
Barbara Mendes studied art throughout her youth in NYC; then published stories and covers in *Underground Comix* under the name "Willy Mendes". She developed her style of brilliantly colored narrative paintings, epic in detail and scale, and has exhibited them in New York, Chicago, Los Angeles, Florida, and Tel Aviv. Her Biblical murals are permanently displayed in Jerusalem and Florida. Her Los Angeles studio/gallery is open to the public; the building features her intricate and blazing outdoor "Angel Mural". The 6 ft. x 16 ft. "Vayikra Mural" (oil-on-canvas, 2009), illuminating each of 859 verses in the Book of Leviticus, is available.

STEVE LEIALOHA
Steve Leialoha is best known for his inking and penciling on Vertigo's *Fables* and illustrating the *Fables* novel *Peter & Max!* Other Vertigo contributions include: *Jack of Fables, Nevada, Petrefax, the Dreaming, Sandman,* and *Dead Boy Detectives*.

Since the mid 70's he was an inker on *Warlock, Howard the Duck, Daredevil,* the *GI Joe* silent issue, *Superman, Batman, Captain Marvel, Ms Marvel, Captain America, The Avengers, Secret Wars II, Fantastic Four,* and the original 1977 *Star Wars* movie adaptation.

For Marvel and DC Comics he has also drawn *Dr Strange, Iron Man, The X-men, New Mutants, Hulk, She-Hulk, Spider-Man, Spider-Woman, The Hitchhiker's Guide to the Galaxy* and *Star Trek*.

KEN STEACY
Ken decided at age eleven to become a professional comic book author/illustrator, a dream he realized in 1974. Since then, he has worked in the industry as writer, artist, art director, editor, and publisher, chronicling the exploits of *Astro Boy, Spider-Man, Harry Potter,* and the *Star Wars* gang, to name but a few. In addition to creating his own intellectual property, he has also collaborated with other writers, including Harlan Ellison and Douglas Coupland.

He is the recipient of an Eisner and an Inkpot award, and in 2009 was inducted into the Canadian Comic Book Hall of Fame, a lifetime achievement award for contributions to the industry. He currently teaches Comics

& Graphic Novels at Camosun College in Victoria BC, a visual storytelling program he co-created with his wife, author/illustrator Joan Steacy.

JOAN STEACY

Joan grew up in southern Ontario, and is a graduate of Sheridan College, The Ontario College of Art & Design, and The University of Victoria. A visual artist who has worked in a variety of disciplines, including sculpture, traditional illustration, and digital imaging, she is the author/illustrator of *So, That's That!*, a biography of her father who lived to be 100 years old.

Her most recent work is *Aurora Borealice*, a trilogy of autobio/graphic novels, the final volume of which is nearing completion. It debuted at the Toronto Comic Arts Festival and was nominated for a Doug Wright Award. She currently teaches Comics & Graphic Novels at Camosun College in Victoria BC, a visual storytelling program she co-created with her husband, author/illustrator Ken Steacy.

SHARY FLENNIKEN

Shary Flenniken is a freelance cartoonist, editor, and screenwriter currently living in Seattle, Washington. She holds degrees in Multimedia Technology and Professional Teaching. She is best known as the creator of the *Trots & Bonnie* comic strip and as a contributor and editor at *National Lampoon Magazine*. She is currently writing and drawing for *American Bystander Magazine*.

SARAH GLIDDEN

Sarah Glidden is a non-fiction cartoonist who lives in Seattle. Her newest book is *Rolling Blackouts*, published by Drawn and Quarterly.

EVE FURCHGOTT

Eve Furchgott is a cartoonist, printmaker and graphic artist. During the '70s and '80s, she lived in San Francisco (where she first met Trina Robbins!) and was the creator of Far Out West, a serial comic strip chronicling her life in a Haight Ashbury commune. Since moving to the Big Island of Hawai'i in the early '90s she has been the illustrator of many children's books of Hawaiian lore and culture. She runs a freelance graphics business, Blue Heron Multimedia, and spends what time she can in her printmaking studio. She is slowly working on an update of *Far Out West*, and is in early stages of a graphic memoir of sorts, tentatively entitled *Dogs I Have Known and Loved*.

ELIZABETH WATASIN

Elizabeth Watasin is the author of the Gothic steampunk series *The Dark Victorian*, *The Elle Black Penny Dreads*, the paranormal sci-fi noir series, *Darquepunk*, and the creator/artist of the indie comics favourite

Charm School, which was nominated for a Gaylactic Spectrum Award. Gentlewoman and artist, respected member of the animation guild with thirteen animated feature film screen credits, she lives in Los Angeles with her black cat named Draw, busy bringing readers uncanny heroines in queer sci-fi, Victorian punk, and diesel fantasy. Winner, Best Lesbian Fantasy & Fantasy Romance, 2015 Rainbow Awards.

ANNE TIMMONS

Anne started her comic art career on a high, illustrating two *Star Trek* stories. Soon after came *Dignifying Science*, a graphic biography of women in science. Anne met Trina at Comic-Con, setting the stage for many and varied collaborations. They first teamed up on *GoGirl!*, the crime fighting teenager who can fly. They also worked together on an illustrated adaption of *Little Women*, and biographies of Florence Nightingale and Hedy Lamarr. Anne also illustrated Trina's award-winning *Lily Renee: Escape Artist*, about the groundbreaking Golden Age comic artist who as a girl escaped Nazi Germany on the Kindertransport.

CARYN LESCHEN

Caryn Leschen is known mostly for her stories in *Wimmin's Comix* and *Twisted Sisters* anthologies. She self-syndicated her comic, *Ask Aunt Violet*, to alternative weeklies all over North America. As principal of Aunt Violet Productions, she draws and designs for web, print, and mobile platforms, specializing in food and travel illustration. Ms. Leschen is also an Adjunct Professor at the University of San Francisco, where she teaches Animation and Drawing on the iPad. She's working on her first graphic novel, *Once a Month Like a Period*, and lectures widely on drawing comics on the iPad, as she considers comics her purest form of self-expression. Learn more at www.auntviolet.com.

JEN VAUGHN

A storyteller in all weather, Jen works by day as a narrative designer for games (*Plants Vs Zombies: Heroes* and *Nicki Minaj: The Empire*) while by night slowly drawing comics with badass women (*Cartozia Tales*, *Avery Fatbottom*, *Backstory*) and knitting for her loved ones.

ROBERT TRIPTOW

Robert Triptow first met Trina Robbins during his editorship of the groundbreaking *Gay Comix* series, inviting her to contribute as a "guest heterosexual." He then co-edited the award-winning *Strip AIDS U.S.A.* with her and Bill Sienkiewicz. Triptow has cartooned for other many underground and alternative titles like *Bizarre Sex*, *Young Lust*, *Real Girl*,

Juicy Mother, The Book of Boy Trouble. His first solo project, *Class Photo*, the life stories of 66 people in a 1937 school picture, was released in 2015.

TERRY LABAN

In his 3 decades as a professional cartoonist, Terry LaBan has drawn political cartoons, created numerous alternative comic book series for Fantagraphics and Dark Horse Comics, written for Donald Duck comics for Egmont and off-putting mature stories for DC Vertigo and spent 15 years co-creating with his wife *Edge City*, a daily syndicated comic strip for King Features. He lives in a leafy suburb of Philadelphia with easy access to numerous synagogues.

MIRIAM LIBICKI

Miriam Libicki is a graphic novelist living in Vancouver, Canada. Her short comics have been published by Alternate History Comics, Rutgers University Press, and the *Journal of Jewish Identities*, and her 2008 Israeli Army memoir "jobnik!" has been used in over a dozen university courses. Her new book of drawn essays, *TOWARD A HOT JEW* was published fall 2016 by Fantagraphics.

MIRIAM KATIN

Miriam Katin, born in Hungary in 1942 immigrated to Israel after the Hungarian uprising in 1956. She apprenticed in a Tel Aviv graphic studio for two years in the 1960s before joining Israel Defense Forces as a graphic artist. With no formal training, she became involved in animation and design working with Ein Gedi Animation, Nickelodeon, MTV Animation, and Disney. Her graphic novel *We Are On Our Own* premiered in 2006 and has won multiple awards since and been translated into six different languages.

TRINA ROBBINS

In 1970, Trina Robbins produced the very first all-woman comic book, *It Ain't Me, Babe*. In 1972 she was one of the founding mothers of *Wimmin's Comix*, the longest-lasting women's anthology comic book. (1972 – 1992)

In the mid-1980s, tired of hearing publishers and editors say that girls don't read comics and that women had never drawn comics, she co-wrote (with catherine yronwood) *Women and the Comics*, the first of what would become a series of histories of women cartoonists. She has been responsible for rediscovering previously forgotten early women cartoonists like Nell Brinkley, Tarpe Mills, and Lily Renee.

In 2013 Trina was inducted into the Will Eisner Comic Book Hall of Fame.

Made in the USA
Columbia, SC
13 July 2019